P9-EEA-862

SUPPLEMENTS / 13

Craving and Salvation

A Study in Buddhist Soteriology

Bruce Matthews

Published for the Canadian Corporation for Studies in Religion / Corporation Canadienne des Sciences Religieuses by Wilfrid Laurier University Press

Canadian Cataloguing in Publication Data

Matthews, Bruce, 1941-
Craving and salvation

(SR supplements ; 13)
Bibliography: p.
Includes index.
ISBN 0-88920-147-1

1. Salvation (Buddhism). 2. Tipiṭaka. Suttapiṭaka – Criticism, interpretation, etc. I. Title. II. Series.

BQ4453.M37 294.3'422 C83-098808-4

© 1983 Corporation Canadienne des Sciences Religieuses/
Canadian Corporation for Studies in Religion

No part of this book may be translated or reproduced in any form, by print, photoprint, microfilm, microfiche, or any other means, without written permission from the publisher.

Cover design by Michael Baldwin, MSIAD

Order from:
Wilfrid Laurier University Press
Wilfrid Laurier University
Waterloo, Ontario, Canada N2L 3C5

AUGUSTANA LIBRARY
UNIVERSITY OF ALBERTA

Victoriae et Harriet

Duabus in Deo sororibus pietate
caritateque excellentibus hoc dedico.

CONTENTS

PREFACE

I acknowledge the assistance and support of many friends and associates in the preparation of this text. Part of the challenge of approaching another religious tradition for analysis and reflection involves meeting with informed and receptive adherents of that tradition. In this regard, I have three individuals to thank for opening up a whole field of scholarly and monastic contacts. These are Dr. Andrew Nanayakkara of Colombo, Mr. Justice U Chan Htoon of Rangoon, and Professor Sulak Sivaraksa of Bangkok.

Closer to home, I have in particular my colleague Professor Hebert Lewis to thank for his fine editorial assistance. Marie-Thérèse McGuinness also helped in this regard. Appreciation is likewise extended to Christine Lenihan and Deborah Seary for typing the manuscript. This book has been published with the help of a grant from the Canadian Federation of the Humanities, using funds provided by the Social Sciences and Humanities Research Council of Canada. Further assistance was received in the form of a Harvey T. Reid grant from Acadia University. And finally for my wife Pam, an expression of gratitude for her patience in seeing me through this lengthy endeavour.

Might I now also alert the reader to the fact that all the translations from the Pāli texts are my own, except where indicated. I have consulted and sometimes used the translations of the Pāli Text Society on occasions where I judged them to be precise and accurate. I have also decided to use the more common Sanskrit spellings of karma and nirvāṇa where those terms appear in my discussion. In the sources they remain, of course, as *kamma* and *nibbāṇa*.

Low Sunday, 1983

FOREWORD

by

Robert Lawson Slater

Whatever else may be said of the one world of today, it is a world whose coming and going includes the coming and going of scholars from various countries interested in other ways of faith besides their own. The fact that Bruce Matthews is such a scholar adds to the value and interest of what he has to say on the subject of Buddhist "craving and salvation," as taught by the Buddha and understood by Theravāda Buddhists in South East Asia as well as by Western scholars like himself.

Beginning with a research visit to Sri Lanka (Ceylon), he has in these last ten years extended his travels to include Burma and Thailand. Thus, he compares conclusions drawn from his own studies of the Pāli texts with conclusions drawn by such scholars as K. N. Jayatilleke and M. W. P. de Silva. What Matthews has to say should lead his readers to review a good many of the conclusions about craving they have drawn from Buddhist texts in the past—and to review some of the Western interpretations of these texts.

They may be the more disposed to examine and reconsider earlier conclusions by what Professor Matthews has to say about the growing Buddhist interest in "unconscious craving," especially if they have been interested in Western presentations of "depth religion."

His description of his essay as "a study of Buddhist soteriology" should lead his readers to look for something more than a swift glance at Buddhist practices, interpretations, and speculations today. They will not be disappointed.

Robert Lawson Slater
Professor Emeritus,
Harvard University

ABBREVIATIONS

A.	Anguttara Nikāya
D.	Dīgha Nikāya
Dhm.	Dhammapada
Itv.	Itivuttaka
M.	Majjhima Nikāya
S.	Saṃyutta Nikāya
Sn.	Suttanipāta
Ud.	Udāna
Thera.	Theragāthā
Theri.	Therīgāthā

INTRODUCTION

This monograph concerns the function of craving in religious life, an absorbing and important issue that confronted the Buddha, and one to which he responded in a creative, singular way. It is a subject which is not always understood by those interested in Buddhist thought. This is so partly because the role craving has in the Buddhist plan of salvation is easy to oversimplify and misinterpret. Thus, many studies do not appreciate the way in which craving is involved with an entire process of will and insight that leads to self-transformation and awareness. Some even go so far as to confound craving with forms of desire and willing which are in fact considered by the Buddha to be "skillful" and conducive to salvation. This common misconception takes the entire range of human want to be something harmful, an interpretation which is not consistent with the facts of either Buddhist scripture or practice.

It can be argued that seeing craving in its correct perspective is strategic to an understanding of what Buddhism is all about. Buddhist doctrine in a single grasp comprehends the psychological dimensions of life and the ordinary experiences of life. Above all, it answers questions of human nature: What is man? How is he constituted? Why is he continually subject to craving? Is there any escape from the awareness of pain and the bonds of an unending cycle of life? Because the Buddhist understanding of salvation is based on such queries, not unexpectedly its response is largely inward. It searches out the source of painfulness deep within the psyche.

Uttered more than two thousand years ago in northern India, this message intuitively seems to us to be contemporary and relevant because of its psychological emphasis. Notwithstanding this, it is also a religious statement in the sense that it demands a decision on the part of anyone who stands at the crossroad of paths which may lead to enlightenment or to persistent ignorance. What the Buddha said about craving is especially pertinent to this. Selfish craving is perceived as an insuperable obstacle to personal equilibrium and liberation. Of this there is no question, and, for one who cares to look seriously, everyday examples of craving are no longer mere coincidences or unrelated psychological phenomena. They are strategic and significant events which grip mankind in continuous rebirth and suffering. Such craving represents a complete way of life which prevents the individual's development: it thwarts the cultivation of good or wholesome desire, and leads towards ever-increasing egocentricity and painfulness. The power of the Buddha's hope, however, lies in the recognition that this state can be changed. So he teaches— "Put aside what is unwholesome. It is possible to do so. If it were not possible...I would not ask you" (A.1.58).[1]

The challenge in analyzing Buddhist psychological theory is to go beyond the formalistic textual data provided in the Pāli literature and to touch upon the verticle or spiritual aspect of this teaching. It is gratifying to see such scholars as Rune Johansson, Winston King, and Padmasiri de Silva[2] pursue excursions into Buddhist psychology which make religious sense. Others such as Robert Ornstein, Herbert Fingarette, and John Dunne[3] make fruitful comparative use of a large range of Buddhist psychological concepts as religious actions, from the process of psychoanalysis to the expansion of consciousness in meditation. Still, there are some who are not so careful. They pick and choose and build up a false sense of the whole.

There are dangers in every exploration of Buddhism. Adopting sound historical and hermeneutical procedures will keep us alert. In the long run it is a matter of interpretation, of where to put emphasis in Buddhist soteriology.[4]

With this in mind I seek to bring to this study not only a critical examination of most of the key canonical texts of the Sutta Piṭaka (Nikāyas)[5] but to exhibit what I take to be the meaning of these texts to Buddhists today. During many periods of residency in Buddhist South and Southeast Asia, particularly Sri Lanka, I have discussed this topic with Theravāda devotees, from learned monks to ordinary villagers. As one might expect with a non-credal religion, there is no single specific interpretation about such a subject as this. Even the texts themselves are equivocal and a reading of them depends on prior belief and interpretive approach.

Methodologically, then, this study examines the concept of craving in Buddhism from both a phenomenological and "religious" perspective.[6] It is not a semantic analysis of the Pāli word *taṇhā* (craving) as such, but an attempt to see exactly what the Buddha meant when he said that to experience was to "burn with thirst" (Itv. 23). I will give a description of the origin, development, and activity of craving as set down chiefly in the Sutta Piṭaka. There is also the more pressing responsibility to interpret this data and give it meaning in the light of contemporary Buddhist understanding.

The first priority is to see how craving is part of a much larger structure, closely related as it is to the central Buddhist concept of painfulness (*dukkha*). Second, it must be shown how painfulness is provoked by the grosser forms of craving. At this point, we must deal with the various mental factors which for traditional Buddhism make up consciousness and unconsciousness. This portion of the analysis brings forward the psychological structure of mankind and demonstrates the individual's potential to control craving. Having established how craving arises, how it affects the mind, and how it can be redirected, I turn to its spiritual implications in a final chapter, whose theme is emancipation. It concludes that a critical dimension of the path to awareness and freedom is conative in scope and involves the engagement and harnessing rather than the suppression of craving. This discussion will round out the inquiry so as to point up the full range and implications of craving as the foremost religious issue in Buddhism.

Chapter 1

CRAVING AND PAINFULNESS

The Buddhist plan of salvation gives craving a prominent place in the Four Noble Truths, one of the most precise articulations of the human condition envisioned by any religion. These truths, as set down in the celebrated first sermon of the Buddha (S.5.420), state simply that life is suffering or painfulness (*dukkha*); that among the several causes (*samudaya*) of painfulness, craving is the most conspicuous; that there is a state in which painfulness is extinguished (*nirodha*); and finally, that a way (*magga*) exists to achieve this liberation.

Seen as a collection of straightforward observations about existence, the Four Truths exhibit a unique chasteness by their economy of expression. Buddhist soteriology is able to touch deeply and meaningfully on profound spiritual issues with brevity and exactness. It is no surprise to find passages in the Sutta Piṭaka which suggest that awareness or liberation is not necessarily the product of a lifetime of meditation and cerebral struggle but can be achieved under conditions of extraordinary simplicity.[1]

The texts are often deliberate in first setting down a teaching without frills or elaboration, suggesting that the alert will immediately perceive its import. The bulk of a *sutta*, or chapter, will, however, be aimed at the less perceptive, who will receive a sometime lengthy and carefully developed homily on the subject at hand.

This is certainly the case with the Four Noble Truths. By themselves they are the mere hint of a landscape, a foreshortening of an entire reality. Within these truths there is room for a complex epistemology, ontology, and metaphysic to unfold, according to one's level of preparation and endeavour. Each truth is invested with an intricacy and subtlety that may at first elude the eye. And yet the paradox remains—for the aware the Four Truths say all that is necessary. It is only for those who still struggle with the forces of egocentricity and passion that the great discourses are set down in detail, the problems of painfulness and its causes elaborated, and the goal of nirvāna brought into focus.

It is in the second truth of *samudaya*, or the arising of painfulness, that the issue of craving is understandably located. But it is not confined by a rigid framework only to that truth. As will become evident, in each truth the other three inevitably have a place, if only to define more clearly the thrust of the truth under discussion. This is the case with the first truth of *dukkha*, to which we now turn.

1. Dukkha

Because it is the first truth, the assertion that "life is painfulness" has for many Westerners become the hallmark of Buddhism. Indeed, Buddhist teachings invite release from the condition of *dukkha*, but as one investigates the Buddhist sense of painfulness it should be acknowledged that, by itself, this is an inadequate description of the Buddha's general outlook. His perspective is balanced by his awareness of the possibilities of equilibrium and inner harmony, of compassion and service for those who care to go beyond themselves.

Dukkha (from *du*—bad, low + *kha*—to be empty, hollow) is hard to translate, as most students of Buddhism discover. Forewarned by T. W. Rhys Davids that no word in English covers the same ground as *dukkha* does in Pāli,[2] one can expect to encounter any number of translations, from the traditional "suffering" and "painfulness" to the more specialized sense of "sadness," "unsatisfactoriness," or even "disharmony."[3] Many naunces are to be found in the word. The Pāli texts, to be sure, are aware of them, and, accordingly, a traditional classification of *dukkha* into three distinct aspects is frequently found (S.4.259; D.3.216; M.2.106). This seemingly arbitrary discernment eventually can be seen to contain the physical, psychological, and existential manifestations of painfulness:

> Painfulness, painfulness! is the saying, friend Sariputta. But what, friend, is painfulness? There are these three forms of painfulness: the sort caused by bodily pain (*dukkha dukkhatā*), the sort caused by psychological change (*sankhāra dukkhatā*),[4] the sort caused by the changeable nature of things (*vipariṇāma dukkhatā*). S.4.259

These three orders of painfulness might be seen as corresponding in many ways to another well-known Buddhist ontological formula, the *ti-lakkhaṇa,* or Three Characteristics of Existence, namely, painfulness, the impermanency of the objective world (*anicca*), and the insubstantiality of the subjective, the specious "self" or "I" (*anattā*). In the Dhammapada (277) a "path to purity" (*maggo visuddhiyā*) that depends upon realizing (*paññāya*) these characteristics is marked out. Here, reluctance to accept their inevitability is equated with the crippling ignorance that fuels further painfulness.

These classifications adumbrate the kinds of suffering the Buddha was intent on coming to grips with. The first, *dukkha dukkhatā*, refers to the uninvited models of physical pain ("racking, sharp and bitter"—"*dukkhaṃ tippaṃ kharaṃ kaṭukaṃ*"; Ud.21). It also accommodates the span of daily anxieties and apprehensions that are a permanent feature of life in a complicated and perturbed world. Most people know, as well, family and domestic crisis. Indeed, some of the most obvious kinds of painfulness are experienced in attachments to loved ones strained and broken by misunderstanding, inability to communicate, and death. In M.2.106 we read of the death of an only son; it leaves the father heartbroken, and we are warned what to expect from parental love: "That is just it, householder. For grief, sorrow, suffering, misery, and despair are born of affection (*piyajātikā*), originate in affection (*piyappabhavikā*)." This tells us that when conditions change, as change they must, what is joy or satisfaction reverses itself. To some the cause of this kind of pain is obvious; they can accept it, and can even learn from it. Others are unaware of the potential for painfulness that lurks behind every disposition and thought. Only the most obvious physical and mental aspects of pain strike them, and, because of ignorance, the causal source and the path to surcease are not realized. Thus, in the Sutta Piṭaka ignorance is aptly defined as not knowing the facts about *dukkha* (M.1.54).

In the second and third classifications of pain the link between pain and flux or momentariness (a crucial Buddhist affirmation) is greatly expanded, and its cosmological implications revealed. *Dukkha* comes to reflect a world-view expressed in the profoundly Indian concept of *saṃsāra*. From its verbal root, *saṃsāra* means "faring" or "travelling on." By the time of the Upaniṣads (ca. 800-500 B.C.) the doctrine of life as a cycle of creation, destruction, and re-creation had become prevalent. A developed sense of karma as a doctrine of moral justice enabled the individual to see his place in the wider scope of *saṃsāra*, giving rise to the idea of rebirth. In some of the earliest Upaniṣadic references to this theme (Chandogya 5.3; Bṛhadāraṇyaka 6.2) there is the conviction that happiness and painfulness are invited by previous action in the present and former existences.

The Buddhist concept of *saṃsāra* expresses similar micro-and macrocosmic concerns found in early Hinduism. Certainly, the unavoidable deterioration of the human condition and long-term worthlessness of desires and sense pleasures are well expressed in both traditions,[5] consistent with the shared witness to contingent change and momentariness (*khaṇika*). The Buddha acknowledges as well the eternal magnitude of *saṃsāra*, perceived as a coil developing from a circle, with no beginning, and with its end not yet in sight, undetermined. Therefore, he teaches: "the earliest point of the faring-on" is not revealed "to beings cloaked in ignorance, tied to craving" (*avijjānīvaraṇānaṃ sattānaṃ taṇhāsaṃyojanānaṃ* - S.2.178). As *saṃsāra* has no beginning, so too there is no end for those still "fettered by craving," who in their ignorance regard the body or any of its attributes as a permanent "self":

> There comes a time, monks, when the mighty ocean dries up, is completely drained, when it no longer comes to be. But of beings impeded by ignorance, fettered by craving, who run on the round of rebirth, I declare no end.
> Monks, just as a dog tied up by a leash to a strong stake or pillar keeps running and revolving around the stake or pillar, even so the untaught persons, who do not discern the noble truth, who are untrained in doctrine, regard body as self, regard feeling, perception, activity, consciousness as having self....
> I declare that they are not released from rebirth, from old age and decay, sorrow and grief, sadness, woe and despair.
> S.3.149

In this passage he who is unenlightened fails to acknowledge that the phenomenal world is held in the embrace of *saṃsāra*. This failure leads to the existential painfulness (*vipariṇāma dukkha*) which comes from placing value and emphasis on the material and transient. Of still greater significance is the teaching that not only is the material state of body in flux (*anicca*), but so is the subjective self, the "personality." This is non-self (*anattā*), and want of acknowledging its status leads to what is perhaps the most persistent and baffling kind of psychological painfulness (*sankhāra dukkha*), painfulness which has its answer concealed within the second noble truth. Here the Buddha teaches that the cause of much suffering is to be found in the persistent reiteration of a sense of "real" personality, in which one locates and anchors himself. This leads to the idea of self as an unchangeable entity. From here everything is judged and valued within the egocentric perspective of craving. And more, by way of the preconceived notion of a permanent ego, there arises a craving for a permanent world with permanent pleasures and gratifications.

Because this is an erroneous account of reality, it gives rise to frustration, disappointment and pain.

The second noble truth is at once a description of man in this state of painfulness and an answer to the question of how this sort of pain arises in the first place.[6] It is true that the Buddha often, and simply, refers to the second truth as "that craving which leads to rebirth" (*yāyaṃ taṇhā ponobbhavikā*, S.5.421). But the second truth points to a cause of painfulness which is far more complex than the phenomenon of craving itself. In accordance with his method of teaching for all levels of cerebral and intuitive comprehension, the Buddha carries the noble truth of craving beyond the commonly accepted statement and further demonstrates to those capable of understanding how craving fits into an intricate description of man. This description is intended to explain the painful state of becoming—the conditioned genesis, growth, development, and decay of the individual. Failure to understand this impermanency provokes its own unique kind of painfulness (*sankhāra dukkha*). What we need to see now are the ways in which this state of "becoming," the conditioned "personality," are described in Buddhism.

2. Personality and Painfulness

> Person! Person! it is said, O venerable sir. But what is it that the Blessed One has called the "person"? M.1.299 [7]

One of the most salient features of Buddhism is that it is built upon a careful analysis of the "person" both in terms of bodily events as well as human conscious and unconscious activity. Painfulness has its obvious origins within this psycho-physical framework. The Buddha teaches that despite the absence of a permanent person there is a conventional self, to be described as a continuity of processes (*santati*) which comprises becoming (*bhava*), birth (*jāti*), ageing, death (*jarāmara*), and re-becoming (*punabbhava*). This is *asmimāna* or the sense of being a self (M.1.139), what later Theravāda tradition refers to as the "conventional" (*sammuti*) as apart from the "ultimate" understanding or acknowledgement of self.[8] Traditionally, Buddhists have a variety of methods to explain the physical and mental factors which make up the "process" or the "person." In the Sutta Piṭaka four approaches were developed, two from a psycho-physical standpoint (*pañcakkhandha* and *paṭicca-samuppāda*) and two from a purely mental focus (*citta* and *mano*). In the present context, which is concerned with the notion of the self in Buddhism, the two psycho-physical descriptions, as synthetic explanations showing the co-relative interdependence of mental and physical factors, are the most useful. In the next chapter, where the aim will be to trace the etiology of craving within the personality, we can concentrate on the process of consciousness (*viññāṇa*) in the *paṭiccasamuppāda*, and on the mental factors of *citta* and *mano*.

3. The *Pañcupādānakkhandhā* (The Five Grasping Groups)

> Your reverences, the matchless wheel of teaching (*dhamma*) set rolling by the Tathāgata, perfected one, fully self-awakened one, in the deer park at Isipatana near Benares cannot be rolled back.... It was a proclamation, a teaching, a laying down, establishing, opening up, analyzing, and making plain of the Noble Truth of painfulness.... And what, your reverences, is the Noble Truth of Painfulness? Birth is pain, ageing is pain, dying is pain, grief, sadness, suffering, misery, and despair are pain. And not getting what one wants, that too is pain. In brief, the Five Groups of Grasping are painfulness (*saṃkhittena pañcupādānakkhandhā dukkhā*). M.3.249

In this text painfulness is summed up, linking it with the modalities of the Five Grasping Groups. And further, the activity of the five groups (*khandhā*) does not take place in a substantive person.[9] When the Buddha refers to these groups as grasping in nature, he means to emphasize how easy it is to cling to a false idea of person when in reality a life is but a process of factors constantly undergoing change.

The five groups are, first, the physical factor of *rūpa*, which is material form or body. In the Sutta Piṭaka, form is described as being made up of four primary modes of solidity, fluidity, heat and motion (M.1.28). But form is not considered as altogether material. Although a distinction can be made between body and mind, the difference between them is only one of degree. Thus, for example, form can also include the function of organic sensations.[10] In order to overcome any suggestion of overt dualism, the term is often joined by the word *nāma*, name (viz. *nāma-rūpa*) "name and form"). In S.2.3, *nāma* is described as sensation, ideation, will, contact and attention. Consisting of certain central psychological functions, name links form with the four other aggregates, the more precise factors of feeling, perception, will and consciousness (*vedanā, saññā, sankhāra* and *viññāṇa*).

Vedanā commonly refers to any kind of mood, feeling, or sensation ("good sensation, unpleasant sensation, neutral sensation"—"*sukhā vedanā dukkha vedanā adukkhamasukhā vedanā*," S.4.232). Some object to the translation "feeling," arguing that the expression "neutral feeling", for instance, does not make sense, or that the broader epistemological meaning of *vedanā* is not adequately expressed. These are cautionary remarks to be respected, but despite possible shortcomings *vedanā* rendered as feeling is still found in most translations.

The third group, *saññā*, means assimilation of sensations or perceptions. It is a key term in Buddhist soteriology—in many ways, the principal factor that either leads to or prevents awareness. A modern psychologist puts this in perspective when he writes, "man is, of all animals, the most voyeuristic. He is more dependent on his visual sense than most animals, and his visual sense contributes more information than any of his senses."[11] But *saññā* is more than just visual perception. It refers to all senses and to the mind, with its memory and imagination ("perceptions are these six: perception of form, sound, smell, taste, touch, and ideas"—"*cha yimā...saññā: rūpasaññā, saddasaññā, gandhasaññā rasasaññā, phoṭṭhabbasaññā, dhammasaññā,*" A.3.413). Buddhism has traditionally placed much emphasis on how we determine the quality of our environment, of the outward world around us. There is a distinct philosophical idealism suggested in such passages as S.1.39: "the world is brought up by the mind, is swept away by the mind"—"*cittena nīyati loko, cittena parikissati*"), suggestive of the vital role perception and ideation play in the appreciation of what is real, true, and good. How one controls perception, then, towards the goal of gaining independence from its grasping, shallow interpretation of objects and events, is crucial to the religious life of harmony and equilibrium.

The fourth or *sankhāra* group will be carefully reviewed in a later context, but it is presently necessary to have some idea of its meaning as one of the Five Grasping Groups. It usually denotes will or volition, although this translation is contentious. This is because the root structure of the word (*saṃ*—together + *kṛ*—to make, to do) suggests that *sankhāra* could mean "conditioned states" rather than will. But as Jayatilleke points out:

> It is of great significance that apart from the traditional exegesis on *sankhāra* in "*aniccā vata sankhārā*", as all "compounded constituents" there isn't a single instance in the Canon of the word being used of a material object or objects compounded of elements...yet it is evident that some translators seemed to have been guided largely by the etymology of the term than by the meaning elicited in its several contexts, and this explains the choice of such terms as "component things, confections, combinations, conformations, compositions, aggregates, compounds, syntheses, etc.".... (These) seem to stray unnecessarily from the central notion of the concept as denoting "will."[12]

This argument is reinforced by such texts as S.3.60, where *sankhāra* is used synonymously with the conative term *cetanā* (will, volition, purposeful striving): "What are the *sankhāra*? They are these six forms of purposeful striving (*chayime...cetanākāyā*): striving for form, for sound, for smell, for taste, for touch, for mental images."

Viññāṇa, the fifth and final group, is a complicated term in its own right and like *sankhāra*, will be examined in detail in the next chapter. Understood as "consciousness," it plays an obvious and crucial role in the psycho-physical structure of the five groups.

It is important to emphasize that these groups are impermanent and in constant flux. They are subject to a law of causation which states that for everything that is caused there must be a prior and different condition ("What is the single doctrine? All beings persist through causes. All beings persist through conditions" —"*Katamo eko dhammo? Sabbe sattā āhāra-ṭṭhitikā, sabbe sattā saṃkhāraṭṭhitikā*," D.3.211). Because the groups arise out of a cause, they cannot be self-existing. Physiologically this is demonstrated in the continuous breakdown and restructuring of the cells, in the fact that nothing in the body, not even nails, teeth or bones, has a permanency in its present state of longer than a few years. And again, from a "mentalistic" perspective, what one may think to be a permanent entity such as "the mind" is in reality a continual flow of sensations, perceptions, volitions, and states of consciousness and unconsciousness. Thus we can concede that the Five Groups constitute a conditioned process ("by reason of a cause it came to be, by rupture of a cause it dies away"—*hetum paṭicca sambhūtaṃ, hetubhaṅgā nirujjhati*," S.1.134), and none of the constituents can exist apart from the others. Even consciousness (*viññāṇa*) is seen to be ultimately dependent upon the physical body:

> This body of mine has form, it is built up of the four elements, it springs from father and mother, it is continually renewed by so much boiled rice and juicy foods, its nature is impermanence, decay

> abrasion, dissolution, and disintegration; and therein is this consciousness of mine, too, resting, for on that does it depend. D.1.76

As a description of what the "self" is, the Five Grasping Groups seems quite complete. They have no permanency, no ultimate reality, and for this reason lead to pain. For the average individual the origins of painfulness may not be immediately apparent. To come to grips with this inadequacy, the Buddha gave an even more intricate description of man and his involvement with painfulness in the well-known formula of the *paṭiccasamuppāda*.

4. The *Paṭiccasamuppāda* (Series of Dependencies)

At the heart of the Buddhist enlightenment stands the *paṭiccasamuppāda* (*paṭicca*—grounded on, *samuppāda*—origin, genesis: "arising on the grounds of a preceding cause," Series of Dependencies). It demonstrates that nothing can originate without being dependent upon something else—and this includes painfulness. This is brought out clearly in S.2.3f, the most comprehensive analysis of the arising of pain in the Buddhist Canon. Having given an elementary outline of painfulness, the Buddha goes on to reveal how in his enlightenment he came to understand it as becoming (*samudaya*), and becoming as a process of cause and effect (*paṭiccasamuppāda*):

> Then to me, monks, came this thought: what now being present changes to decay and death? Thinking about this with great penetration (*yoniso*), there came this insight: let there be birth, then there is decay and death. Decay and death is conditioned (*paccayā*) by birth. Then to me came this thought: what now being present does birth come to be? What conditions birth? S.2.10

The text goes on to list the traditional factors or "spokes" (*nidānā*) of this well-known formula, working backwards from birth through becoming, grasping, craving, sensation, contact, the sense functions, personality, consciousness, unconscious volition, and ignorance. The recital ends with a sentence which points to its centrality in Buddhist doctrine:

> Coming to be! Coming to be! (*Samudayo samudayo*). At that thought, monks, there arose in me, in things not learned before vision, there arose in me knowledge, insight arose, wisdom arose, light arose.[13]

It should be made clear that the Series of Dependencies has a versatile role in Buddhist thought. This fact has confused some Western scholars, who have tried to defend a limited meaning for the formula. Thus A. B. Keith argued that the *paṭiccasamuppāda* was only an "explanation of misery; it tells us nothing regarding the physical causes," an opinion endorsed by others as well.[14] Others emphasize the causal focus of the formula. So, George Grimm sees the series as an explanation of how the "inscrutable essence" of man comes to the world, to "the realm of not-self (*anattā*)," how he has got into this world of "becoming."[15] T. W. Rhys Davids also stresses the causal theme of the *paṭiccasamuppāda* but points out that it is likewise an answer to the arising of painfulness, an argument he defends by recourse to many textual sources.[16] He is supported by K. N. Jayatilleke, who argues that the formula gives "a causal account of the factors operating in maintaining the process of the individual and thereby of suffering" as well as being employed "to substitute an empirical causal explanation of the (relative) origin and development of the individual in place of an explanation in terms of metaphysical first causes or final causes."[17]

It is evident that in the Sutta Piṭaka the Series of Dependencies answers to the problem of the origin of painfulness, and is likewise a description of the psychophysical and causal structure of human life. In this way it is a microcosmic picture of *saṃsāra*, of each "wheel of life" (*bhavacakka*) that arises and passes away. It can also be averred that part of the *paṭiccasamuppāda* is the most detailed structural concept of mind in the Sutta Piṭaka. The term has, then, a variety of "metaphysical" and psychological functions in Buddhist thought.

The Series of Dependencies was not a fixed model in early Buddhism. This is demonstrated in the wide variation of this formula found in the Sutta Piṭaka. Traditionally the formula begins with ignorance (*avijjā*) and ends with old age and death (*jarāmara*). Between these spokes are ten causal factors. Thus ignorance[18] is said to condition (*paccaya*) volition (*sankhāra*). Volition, conditioned by the illusion of selfhood (egoism), produces consciousness (*viññāṇa*), which in turn conditions name and form of "personality" (*nāmarūpa*). Name and form condition the six bases of sense cognition (*saḷāyatana*), and the senses condition the quality of impressions (*phassa*). *Phassa* is the stimulus that provokes a wide variety of mental activities, approximating the function of *saññā* ("perceptions," as found in the Five Grasping Groups).[19] Through this factor feelings or sensations (*vedanā*) arise, and these, along with previous conditioning causes, further condition craving and are engaged as instruments of craving (*taṇhā*). Craving then provokes entanglement or grasping (*upādāna*), a state which in turn conditions a process of becoming (*bhava*) in conformity to the individual's pattern of conditioned background. *Bhava* is, in effect, the accumulation of energy that leads to new life. From becoming results birth (*jāti*), with its inevitable sequence of old age and death.[20]

This format is not always invoked. Sometimes the causal process is described as beginning, not ending, with old age and death (M.1.49). In other texts the sequence is frequently shortened to only a few of the traditional factors. Thus M.1.38 omits the usual first six and starts with feelings (*vedanā*), and in M.1.256, *taṇhā* (craving) is listed first. Again, one factor may at times receive more attention than others. For example, craving may be further outlined as sensuous craving (*kāmataṇhā*), craving for life and egoistic pursuits (*bhavataṇhā*), and craving for destruction (*vibhavataṇhā*); or, grasping may be described as grasping for sensual pleasure (*kāmupādāna*), grasping for theories (*diṭṭhupādāna*), grasping for customs and rituals (*sīlabbatupādāna*), and grasping in a belief of the soul and substance (*attavādupādāna*). Occasionally the sequence of causes is arranged to emphasize one factor as the key to the end of painfulness (*taṇhā* in S.4.86 and M.1.256). It is not uncommon to find only one of the factors mentioned as the cause of painfulness (for instance, ignorance, M.1.54; consciousness, S.2.13; and craving S.5.420).

The important point here is that the Series of Dependencies has no single first cause. What it describes is a cyclical wheel of life based on a schema of cause and effect, with no real beginning and no end in sight. Wherever and whenever the wheel turns there will be painfulness.

5. The Significance of the Concept of Consciousness in the *Paṭiccasamuppāda*

It has already been suggested that the *paṭicca-samuppāda* or Series of Dependencies is not merely a description of man in a state of painfulness. It also contains within it the answer to the problem of pain. It does this by showing how consciousness directly contributes to states of painfulness. Although the Series of Dependencies like the Five Grasping Groups shows how the mind and physiological functions of the body co-exist in one framework, it can be argued that, unlike the Five Grasping Groups, the central emphasis of the Series of Dependencies is found in its sophisticated theory of consciousness. Rune Johansson brings this point into relief:

> In spite of this dependence (between mind and body), the bodily processes are not further analysed, and the conscious phenomena are always treated as the most important. This may be one of the reasons why the Series of Dependencies (*paṭiccasamuppāda*) often seems to mention things in the wrong order. We are, for instance, used to consider needs as more basic than consciousness, and to interpret consciousness as depending on per-

> ception and perception as depending on the sense organs. Buddhist thinking seems to have started from what is immediately given and most important to the person, namely activity and consciousness. The relations of the rest is [sic] to a great extent implication and activation.[21]

If Johansson is correct, and we will argue more fully in the next chapter that he is, then consciousness in the *paṭiccasamuppāda* should be regarded as more than just an accumulation of mental phenomena. It is a process involving sensory perception, impressions, feelings, and craving. Apart from the psychological importance of this theory, its soteriological import cannot be overestimated. The world in itself ought not to be viewed as either a source of pain or not a source of pain. It is only our relation to it through consciousness that makes it thus or otherwise. Therein lies the key to the Buddha's teaching of deliverance. The average man (*puthujjana*) accepts and relies upon what his senses tell him about the world. In his ignorance (*avijjā*) he is unaware of the momentariness (*khaṇika*) and impermanency not only of the material world (*anicca*), but of his own self (*anattā*). His senses, telling him that ice is cold or that sand is granular, are inadequate because they present information which is pertinent only to the illusory ego. The selfish attitude towards the ego is the basis for craving and attachment. Consequently we do not perceive the material world without fixing egocentric values to it. Attachment to a possession, to another person or object, or even to a doctrine, is to affix that entity to me as mine, or yours, or ours. This can only bring painfulness. It is not possible to satisfy attachments to momentary events.

The aim of Buddhist soteriology is to eradicate attachment and the false sense of self by mastery both of consciousness and the thirsting forces that lie within and behind them. An understanding of the Series of Dependencies makes this liberation possible ("he who sees the nature of *paṭiccasamuppāda* sees the law (*dhamma*), and he who sees the law sees *paṭiccasamuppāda*" M.1.191). Liberation dissolves egocentricity, craving, and subsequent painfulness:

> In so far as a monk, Sariputta, has in this body together with consciousness no tendency (*anusayā*) to the conceit "I" or "mine," and abides in the attainment of that mind's release, of that release through insight—such a monk, Sariputta, has cut off craving, has broken the bonds, has by perfect comprehension of conceit (*mānābhisamayā*) made an end of painfulness. A.1.133

In sum, an investigation of the central Buddhist issue of painfulness has revealed, first, that the tools of inquiry are contained within the second noble truth, the cause for the arising of painfulness. Second, given various expressions of phenomenological, psychological, and existential painfulness in the Sutta Piṭaka, they are best understood by regarding them in the perspective of the Buddhist understanding of flux (*khaṇika*, *saṃsāra*) and by tracing out their causal backgrounds. This is essential for overcoming that kind of painfulness associated with false notions of personality or self. To explain the self and how it generates personality, we looked at early Buddhist psycho-physical descriptions of man, the Five Grasping Groups, and the Series of Dependencies. Of these, the Series of Dependencies gave the most detailed causal picture of self and the arising of painfulness. This formula also yields a theory of consciousness, a theory declared to be the heart of the Series of Dependencies and the key to the problem of pain. In Buddhist psychology consciousness reflects an entire orientation towards the self and the world. For the average individual, "self" and "world" proceed from a consciousness warped and controlled by craving. It is therefore of strategic soteriological importance for the unaware to see how craving is involved in the process of consciousness.

This conclusion leads directly to the issues of the next chapter. Before us we have a profile of man open to various aspects of painfulness. These are fundamentally psychological, and they have their genesis in craving. Craving in the Series of Dependencies and in other descriptions of the mind, notably *mano*, *citta* and *sankhāra*, now have to be brought forward in greater detail.

Chapter 2

MIND AND CRAVING

How does craving arise within the mind? What positive or deleterious effects will it have on the individual? To begin, the concept of consciousness in the Series of Dependencies must be considered in greater detail, particularly the term *viññāṇa* and other factors, including craving, which are closely related to it. Second, what is to be understood by the terms "mind" (*mano* or *mana*), often interpreted as an inner sense with an active instrumental function, and *citta*, which also means mind, but which has an experiential function all its own. Lastly, there is the question of the unconscious. Here the Buddha argues that behind conscious craving there are unconscious roots and inclinations which must be penetrated and controlled if craving itself is to be mastered. Examining these areas will provide an inclusive picture of the Buddhist account of "mind," as well as an understanding of how craving grows and operates within it.

1. *Viññāṇa* as "Consciousness"

In Buddhism the most common Pāli term for consciousness is *viññāṇa*. But how is craving related to this factor? The basic problem here is that of interpreting what the Buddhists mean by *viññāṇa* employed as consciousness, and as the term occurs elsewhere. For, apart from its role in the Series of Dependencies, *viññāṇa* is also used in two other quite different contexts—as a factor in meditation and as the element which "survives" in rebirth.

The first task is to set down the central texts which explain what *viññāṇa* is and how it involves craving. They show that craving is, in fact, part of a whole process of consciousness and not a separate and isolated phenomenon within consciousness.

The principal function of consciousness is stressed in M.1.292:

> Your reverence, it is called *viññāṇa*, *viññāṇa*. Now in what respects, your reverence, is it called *viññāṇa*? Your reverence, it is called *viññāṇa* because it notices (*vijānāti*). And what does it notice? It notices pleasure, pain, and neutral feelings. If it is said it notices, your reverence, there it is called *viññāṇa*.

At M.1.53 a further listing of six kinds of noticing or awareness ("*cha...viññāṇakāyā*") is developed: "becoming aware" through the visual, auditory, olfactory, gustatory, tactile, and mental processes. This dilation emphasizes the close relationship between *viññāṇa* as consciousness and the senses.

The question of how closely this consciousness depends upon and is related to other mental events can only be determined by interpreting the role it plays in the Series of Dependencies. There is controversy over the question of the relation consciousness has with the factors following it in the formula. This has produced two different responses in modern Buddhist psychological studies. Some say that consciousness should be understood apart from the other factors of the series and be rigidly interpreted only as awareness or sensation. Others argue that the function of consciousness in the series cannot be adequately explained apart from the associated factors. It helps to look at a Sutta Piṭaka text to see what these two schools of thought have to say about consciousness. One such text is found in M.1.111:

> Your reverences, in regard to that sermon which the Blessed One recited in brief .... "Whatever the origin, monk, of the number of obsessions and perceptions which assail a man...they are stopped without remainder," of that sermon recited by the Blessed One in brief but whose meaning was not explained in full,

> I understand the meaning in full thus: Dependent on the eye and material forms arises visual consciousness (perception - *cakkuviññāṇam*) the meeting of the three is sensory contact, dependent on contact is feeling, what one feels (*vedeti*) one recognizes (*sañjānāti*), what one recognizes one thinks about (*vitakketi*), and what one thinks about obsesses (deludes or "makes one open to conceptual proliferation" - *papañceti*) one....[1]

How are we to understand the noun *viññāṇa* in this paragraph? E. R. Saratchandra claims that, because *viññāṇa* comes before feeling (*vedanā*) and recognition (*saññā*)[2] in the causal process, *viññāṇa* can mean no more than sensation. He finds the interpretation of *viññāṇa* as a general term for sense consciousness to be too broad and misleading. Thus he writes, "when (*viññāṇa*) came to be applied to the psychology of perception, it meant not full cognition, but bare sensation, a sort of anoetic sentience that occurs before the object is compleely comprehended."[3]

Other contemporary Buddhist scholars, notably K. N. Jayatilleke and Rune Johansson, argue that *viññāṇa* has a much broader meaning when viewed, as it must be, in conjunction with other factors of the Series of Dependencies. So Jayatilleke suggests that in the foregoing citation *viññāṇa* is best translated as perception; but it should be understood that *vedanā* (feelings), *saññā* (recognition), and *viññāṇa* (consciousness) arise simultaneously to give this meaning of perception.[4] Feelings and recognition are, accordingly, directly involved in the function of consciousness.

Johansson supports Jayatilleke in that he too sees a close relationship between consciousness and several of the ensuing factors in the Series of Dependencies. But Johansson goes even further. He develops a unique and plausible argument in the theory of a "*viññāṇa* process." This postulates that there is a process of consciousness in the Series of Dependencies which includes consciousness, "personality," perception, stimulation, feelings, and craving (*viññāṇa*, *nāmarūpa*, *saḷāyatana, phassa, vedanā,* and *taṇhā*). "All these factors in the centre of the series," he writes, "are certainly not causal; they are rather a further analysis of the *viññāṇa*-process, and the arrangement is one of implication and correlation rather than causality."[5] For Johansson, then, the "becoming aware" function of *viññāṇa* is described in terms of process rather than as entity ("from the arising of unconscious volition, *viññāṇa* arises; from the stopping of unconscious volition, *viññāṇa* stops," M.1.53). This reading is reinforced in M.1.256, where *viññāṇa* is described as "named according to whatever condition it arises through" ("if *viññāṇa* arises dependent on eye and forms, it is called eye - *viññāṇa*"), and in the frequent occurrence of the expression "*viññāṇa-sotaṃ*" ("the stream or flow of *viññāṇa*" D.3.105).

This monograph argues that Jayatilleke and Johansson are justified in their claims about the relationship consciousness has with subsequent factors in the Series of Dependencies. Saratchandra's notion that the traditional cause and effect sequence of factors in the series prevents *viññāṇa* from bearing a developed sense of consciousness seems to reflect an excessively mechanistic view of the sequence. His argument, that because *viññāṇa* always comes before perception and feelings in the Series of Dependencies, is a weak one because that sequence is not followed in all the texts. The Series of Dependencies has several different sequences of factors, as has already been pointed out. In some passages perception and feelings come before *viññāṇa*, as, for example, in M.1.293 ("whatever one feels, that one perceives; whatever one perceives, that one is conscious of"—"*yaṃ...vedeti taṃ sañjānāti, yaṃ sañjānāti taṃ vijānāti*"). Certain texts point to a relationship between consciousness and other factors of the Series of Dependencies which make them virtually interchangeable. Thus M.1.293 also states:

> Your reverence, that which is feeling, and that which is perception and that which is consciousness—are these states related or unrelated (*visaṃsaṭṭhā*)? And

> is it possible to lay down a difference between these states, having analyzed them repeatedly?
>
> That which is feeling, your reverence, and that which is perception and that which is consciousness—these states are related, not unrelated, and it is not possible to discriminate (*na... vinibbhujitvā*) between these states, having analyzed them repeatedly. Your reverence, whatever one feels, that one perceives; whatever one perceives, that one discriminates; therefore these states are related, not unrelated, and it is not possible to lay down a difference between these states, having analyzed them repeatedly.

Still other examples emphasize the support collateral factors lend to consciousness. D.3.228 illustrates this kind of relation between consciousness and perception,[6] and in S.2.114 the relation between consciousness and "personality" (*nāmarūpa*) is compared to two bales of reeds supporting each other:

> Your reverence, just as two bundles of reeds (*dve naḷakalāpiyo*) were to stand one supporting the other, even so consciousness is dependent on "personality," and "personality" is dependent on consciousness...thus is the arising of the entire mass of painfulness. But, your reverence, if one of those two bundles of reeds is drawn out, the other one would fall down, and if the latter is drawn, the former one will fall down. Even so, your reverence, with the cessation of consciousness, "personality" ceases.... Thus comes to be the cessation of this entire mass of painfulness.

We have seen how consciousness and the factors of personality, sensory impressions, and feelings can be interpreted as arising simultaneously to support one another, making consciousness part of a process involving several factors at once. The central question now comes forward: is there any evidence that craving (*taṇhā*) is also part of this process?

Johansson has argued that craving is part of a "*viññāṇa* process." The principal text in support of this interpretation is S.4.86. In this description of a Series of Dependencies *viññāṇa* and *taṇhā* are described as the beginning and end of a sequence that, Johansson maintains, should be understood not so much in terms of causality, but as one of "implication," for the factors are "correlative" to each other (i.e., so related that each implies or complements the other):

> Depending on eye and forms arises eye-consciousness (*cakkhuviññāṇaṃ*)—[the text repeats the same about the other senses and their objects]. The coming together of the three is stimulation (*tiṇṇaṃ saṅgati phasso*). Depending on stimulation is feeling. Depending on feeling is craving. But by complete ceasing of craving comes ceasing of becoming. By ceasing of becoming comes ceasing of birth. By the ceasing of birth comes the ceasing of old age and death, of sorrow and grief, of painfulness, of sadness and despair.

Commenting on the "*viññāṇa* process" he sees in this text, Johansson writes:

> From the modern point of view it seems very logical to start with the sense processes: the objects, the sense-organs and the processes of stimulation. That these stimulations are received and evaluated in terms of feelings, is also good psychology. The needs and desires are nowadays considered to be as basic facts as the sense-processes, and they would not be placed in a dependent position by modern psychology, but the Buddhist way of thinking can also be accepted. From the Buddhist point of view it is very significant, that the formulation changes on this point, because the desires are the great problem, and the series goes on to explain that rebirth is stopped if desire is stopped.[7]

In Johansson's judgment craving is the terminal factor in a process of consciousness which begins with *viññāṇa*. This is a sound argument, yet it does not give us enough of an indication of the strategic role craving plays in this process.

The texts on the "four foods" (*cattāro āhārā*, cf. D.3.228; S.2.11, 98, 101; M.1.256) illustrate the dynamic role craving has in its relation to consciousness. These passages further point out that from another perspective craving stands behind the operation of consciousness and to a large extent regulates and manages it. Unlike craving's role seen in S.4.86 above, where craving comes at the end of a process of consciousness, here it describes the genesis of consciousness. These accounts may appear to be inconsistent, but, as pointed out, the sequence of factors in the Buddhist theory of causality is a flexible one. Whether craving is seen in one case as the end of the process of consciousness or as its origin in another, it is significant that in both examples craving is responsible for becoming (*bhava*), and consciousness is taken to be the instrument of furthering this becoming.

Turning to the analogy of the "foods," M.1.261 points out that they are ordinary food (*kabaḷiṃkāra*), sensory stimulation (*phassa*), volition (*manosañcetanā*), and consciousness (*viññāṇa*). Each has craving as its source. In another text which refers to the "four foods" (S.2.98 ff.) the arising of painfulness is traced to craving for any of the foods. But craving alone cannot initiate painfulness. It requires the vehicle of consciousness to activate the wheel of becoming and rebirth. When there is craving for any of the foods, consciousness is firmly placed (*patiṭṭhitaṃ*) and becomes fruitful (or grows—*virūḷham*). The passage ends with two lengthy but helpful analogies which bring this into perspective:

> Monks, it is just as if a dyer or a painter, if there be dye, or lac, or turmeric, or indigo or crimson paint, or a finely polished plank or wall or strip of cloth, can make a woman's or a man's shape complete in all its parts, even so, if there be passion, delight or craving as to ordinary food (or any of the other three), there is consciousness, being firmly placed and fruitful (*evam eva kho bhikkave kabaḷiṃkare ce āhāre atthi rāgo atthi*

> *nandi atthi taṇhā patiṭṭhitaṃ tattha viññāṇaṃ virūḷhaṃ*), "personality" arises, volitions grow, and in the future is becoming and rebirth, grief, despair and trouble.
>
> Monks, it is further just as if there were a house or wall having windows on the north, or the south or the east. When at sunrise a stream of light enters the window, where does it fall upon? "On the west wall, lord." If there be no ground, monks, where does it fall? "On water, lord." If there be no water, monks, where does it fall? "It falls nowhere, lord." Monks, even so if there be no passion, no delight, no craving as to any of the four foods, there consciousness is not placed or is fruitful, there volition does not grow, there in the future is no becoming and rebirth, nor decay and death, grief, despair, and trouble. S.2.102

Now there is a need to examine the two other aspects of consciousness specified at the beginning of this section. We still lack a clear understanding of how consciousness and craving are involved with the rebirth factor of becoming (*bhava*). And there is also the demand of understanding why Buddhists place such strong emphasis on the correct development of consciousness (and therefore with all the dynamic factors involved in the arising of consciousness) in their pursuit of nirvāṇa. Although the soteriological significance of this latter function of consciousness will be set forth in the next chapter, this perspective, at least in outline, must be provided at this point.

2. Craving, Consciousness, and Rebirth

The Theravāda Buddhist theory of causality affirms that a process of consciousness contributes to a state of "becoming" in the next life. But this does not mean that a self or soul transmigrates in the form of consciousness, nor that consciousness proceeds from life to life without change of identity (*anañña*).[8] The question now to be asked: if consciousness is not the equivalent of a soul, how is it a vehicle or agency that transmits an accumulation of its own energy[9] and the deeds of previous lives (*kamma*) into new life (*bhava*)?

Some scholars think that the idea of consciousness as an agency of transmigration is a later one, that it is not compatible with the "empirical" emphasis of the function of consciousness in the Series of Dependencies. Saratchandra, for example, thinks that consciousness as a "transmigrating factor" is a later metaphysical view which came about because of a "gap in the original teaching" and because of the "influence of the Brahmanical factor" under which this new idea was fostered. He further suggests that the Buddha left no statement about this.[10] There are problems with this argument. Jayatilleke has demonstrated that one cannot assume that there was a prevalent belief in reincarnation during the Buddha's lifetime.[11] Furthermore, Saratchandra's contention that the Buddha left no statement about consciousness and rebirth is not consistent with the usual reading of the Sutta Piṭaka. One can agree with Saratchandra in his concern lest consciousness be wrongly assumed to have soul (*attan*) properties, that it might be misinterpreted as a kind of spiritual entity which subsists unchanged from life to life. Clearly, consciousness (*viññāṇa*) is not soul in the *attan* sense. On this point Buddhists concur with Saratchandra. But this does not necessarily imply that consciousness is not involved with rebirth.

Many texts indicate a relationship between sciouness and becoming or "birth" (*bhava*). In Sn. 1055 one is urged not to set his consciousness on becoming ("*viññāṇaṃ bhave na tiṭṭhe*"). In S.2.13 consciousness is cited as the direct cause of rebirth ("the food called *viññāṇa*...is the cause of renewed becoming, of birth in the future"—"*viññāṇahāro... punabbhavābhinibbattiyā paccayo*"). In M.2.262 we are introduced to the unusual term *saṃvattanika* (from *saṃvattati*—"conducive to, involving") *viññāṇa*, which

Wijesekera translates as "the survival factor,"[12] and Horner as "evolving consciousness."[13] From this text alone it can be argued that consciousness evolves after dying, that its causal energy is not checked except in nirvāṇa.

Another way of looking at the role of consciousness in the process of rebirth is to see how it is related to karma (*kamma*). In Buddhism karma has a distinct volitional aspect which prevents it from being the deterministic doctrine some may think it is.[14] Thus it comes to indicate the thought or intention behind a deed or action, as well as the deed itself. Not unexpectedly, in this way craving has a role in determining how karma evolves, how it affects consciousness and thereby the quality of rebirth. In a key text (A.1.223) consciousness, karma, and craving are seen to function together:

> *Kamma* is the field (*khettaṃ*), consciousness the seed (*bījaṃ*), craving the moisture (*sineho*). Of beings that are hindered by ignorance, fettered by craving, consciousness gets support in low (*hīnāya*) conditions.

Here karma, consciousness, and craving are pointed up as the factors essential to rebirth. Craving has an evident dynamic role as the ingredient or "moisture" which nourishes the "seed" of consciousness. Under certain conditions it is presumed that the seed will flower and produce additional seed in an unbroken process of regeneration.

And how does karma fit into this picture? As the "field" in which the "seed" of consciousness grows, the simile suggests that karma is the soil necessary for consciousness to evolve from. Put in psychological terms, the soil represents past lives, intentions, deeds, and actions which provide the background for the arising of consciousness.

In another passage (S.2.82), consciousness is also said to be conditioned by the quality of actions: "If an ignorant man performs an act of merit, consciousness becomes pure (*puññūpagaṃ hoti viññāṇaṃ*). If he performs an act of demerit, consciousness becomes impure." Actions of merit or demerit, whether of speech, thought or behaviour, are also said to make up karma, and this in turn affects rebirth: ("I say, beings are heirs to action"—"*Kammadāyādā sattā ti vadāmi*," M.1.390). It can be argued, therefore, that consciousness carries or transmits its own energy (S.2.97; 4,86) as well as the merits or demerits of acts (S.2.82), and that these proceed from one phenomenal existence to another.

Difficult questions still need to be asked about the process of rebirth. How does consciousness act as an agency in rebirth between one life and another, still within the framework of the Series of Dependencies? How does it do so without violating the fundamental non-self (*anattā*) doctrine of Buddhism? The answer to these questions is found in the factor of grasping or *upādāna*.

3. The Link of *Upādāna*

Upādāna (grasping, clinging, attachment, from *upādiyati*—"to take hold of") is traditionally the ninth spoke in the twelve-fold sequence of the Series of Dependencies. From the viewpoint of cause and effect, it follows craving, which, as we have seen, is the last factor of the "consciousness process." Coming as it does just before becoming or production (*bhava*), grasping is crucial in the process of rebirth. In this capacity it is seldom understood because, at first glance, there may not appear to be any real difference between craving and grasping. It could be maintained, for instance, that grasping as expressed in its conventional four-fold typology ("grasping after sense pleasures, speculative views, customs, and the self"—"*kāmupādānaṃ diṭṭhupādānaṃ sīlabbatupādānaṃ attavādupādānaṃ*," M.1.51; S.23) is only a somewhat stronger form of greed than craving (*taṇhā*), and therefore just as much a part of the process of consciousness as craving. But in the Series of Dependencies, *upādāna* has a more subtle role than is indicated by its English rendering as grasping. It is traditionally listed as the link between the "consciousness process" and becoming. Based on its place in the list alone, Johansson points out that it is possible to interpret *upādāna* as a kind of "emotional investment" in an object which determines the nature of rebirth.

This is a credible interpretation, but it fails to emphasize the most significant feature of the word *upādāna*: the root structure of the noun as *upa* + *a* + *da* means the "substratum by which an active process is kept alive or going." In D.1.45 and, even more significantly, in S.4.399, becoming is compared to a fire wanting fuel (*upādāna*) for combustion.[15] At the end of the passage this fuel is identified as none other than craving itself (*taṇhupādānaṃ*), the foundation of becoming:

> Just as a fire with fuel blazes up, but not without fuel, even so do I declare rebirth to be for him who has fuel, not for him who is without fuel.... At a time when a being lays aside this body and rises up again in another body, for that I declare craving to be the fuel. Indeed, craving is at that time the fuel.[16]

As the link of fuel conditioning rebirth, in one sense grasping belongs more to the new life (*bhava*) than to the old, which generated rebirth. On the other hand, because grasping is the fuel of craving, it must be presumed that this craving is none other than the *taṇhā* of the old "consciousness process." It is the fuel of craving therefore that is the bridge between consciousness and rebirth, the means by which karma and the energy of consciousness proceed into new becoming. Without craving there is no fuel, no basis upon which another life can evolve. Moreover, Buddhists argue that there is nothing metaphysical about the role of consciousness as the agency of rebirth, for it performs this task through the empirical factors of craving and grasping. What passes over in becoming is not a soul (*atta* or *attan*) but a force, a dynamic energy made manifest through craving and karmic volition.

Perhaps the most striking feature of the rebirth process is the central role craving has in necessitating or provoking it, as well as in transmitting the energy that characterizes rebirth. In this way craving takes on an importance not just in the present life but in the whole structure of *saṃsāra*. We can say with confidence that, more than any other factor, craving "turns the wheel."

4. Consciousness, Craving, and Meditation

The subject of consciousness and meditation will be extensively taken up in chapter three. We need now to prepare for some of those observations so as to obtain a deeper understanding of the consciousness factor. It is now clear that consciousness (*viññāṇa*) acts as the carrier of those energies which flow over into the new life. The Sutta Piṭaka also tells us that if consciousness is calm, if it is stopped (Sn. 734, D.1.223), it no longer can flow over, and so in its stabilized condition the consciousness processes "go home" (Ud.93), just as the aware one (*arahant*) "goes home" to the "unconditioned" when the fuel of the Five Grasping Groups is consumed.

This points to an important feature of Buddhist soteriology—that salvation from the wheel of the consciousness process is found in the process itself. By judicious use of consciousness one overcomes ignorance and craving. This gains release from the wheel of rebirth. Consciousness itself is the instrument of its own purification. Training it to be even and orderly, and eventually to extinguish consciousness altogether, is the rationale of meditation. Such an undertaking forces consciousness to assume greater orderliness by relying less and less on its cognitive and conceptual functions. As M.3.223 points out:

> A monk should investigate (things) in such a way that his consciousness (*viññāṇa*), as he investigates, is not scattered and confused (*avikkhittaṃ*) and also not diffused (*avisaṭaṃ*). And without fuel, as he is without longing, there shall be no arising in the future of painfulness resulting from birth, old age and death.

What does this tell us about consciousness? First, that consciousness is tied up with craving, with the fuel that leads to rebirth. And second, that in spite of this fact control of consciousness results in consumption of this fuel. To explain this further, we are elsewhere told (M.1.293, D.1.68f; 3.253) that this control is to be best understood as a series of mental exercises taking place at various levels of meditational awareness (*jhānani* or *jhāna*), levels that for the most part "reside in places of consciousness" (*viññāṇaṭṭhiti*). This is important for it shows that consciousness accompanies all but the last of nine meditational states. Thus, it is possible to argue that, in the first level, consciousness assumes the function of reasoning (*vitakka*) and investigation (*vicāra*). As the levels of meditational awareness advance, the "reasoning" powers of consciousness are more and more nullified and transcended. When the fifth stage is entered, experiences based on perception and cognitive ideas are neutralized. Here oneness of mind with the infinite is developed:

> The monk, by passing beyond the perception of form, by putting an end to sense reaction, by paying no attention to perceptions of diversity, thinks, "the space is infinite," and reaches up to and remains in the mental state of infinite space, (*ākāsānañcāyatanaṃ upasampajja viharati*). D.1.183

The meditator then passes beyond infinite consciousness (*viññāṇanañcāyatana*) to the mental state of nothingness (*ākiñcaññāyatana*), where *viññāṇa* as conscious activity dependent on the senses ceases. This plane, which knows that there is "nothing at all," is realized only by a purified consciousness without the five senses, as is noted in M.1.293:

> Friend, what is knowable by purified consciousness (*viññāṇa*) of the "inner sense" (*mano*) without use of the five sense organs? Thinking, "space is unlimited," the plane of unlimited space is knowable by the clear consciousness of the inner sense without use of the five sense organs; thinking "consciousness is unlimited," the plane of unlimited consciousness is knowable; thinking, "there is nothing at all," the plane of emptiness is knowable.

In an eighth state in which there is neither perception nor non-perception (*nevasaññānāsaññāyatana*), the meditator experiences or feels (*vedanā*) that the consciousness of nothingness has ceased (*ākiñcaññayatanasañña niruddhā hoti*). Only in the ninth and final level of awareness, where consciousness of perception and experience are extinguished (*saññāvedayitanirodha*), does *viññāṇa* not function, and the notion of wisdom (*paññā*, about which there is much to say in the next chapter) is introduced to transcend it:

> And presently, Ananda, passing wholly beyond the mental state of neither perception nor non-perception, I entered and sojourned in the cessation of perception and feeling, and I saw by wisdom that the cankers (*āsavā*) were completely destroyed.
> A.4.448

In closing these remarks concerning consciousness and its relation to craving, a summary of the argument elicits two prominent results. The first conclusion is that *viññāṇa* as a process of consciousness is involved with other dynamic agencies such as perception, feeling, and craving. The combination of different factors produces the force usually termed consciousness, a consciousness which accompanies every perception and feeling. Craving is a constant stimulus to consciousness; it is food for consciousness; and it is the fuel for rebirth. This is clearly demonstrated in the Sutta

Piṭaka, as is the fact that, when consciousness ceases at the zenith of meditation, those cravings which work through it, and the experience of painfulness, also cease.

The psychological picture, then, is that of a process of consciousness closely attached to the world of the senses yet which is nonetheless governed by intention in the form of craving, or lack of it. The dimension of intention directly affects the quality of that consciousness. This perspective evokes the second conclusion: *viññāṇa* is also to be regarded as the medium of the law of rebirth, and thus is the instrument of its own salvation.

The picture is not yet complete. Two other psychological terms related to *viññāṇa*, *citta* and *mano*, need investigation. This can be illustrated by the passage S.2.94:

> Yet this, monks, that we call *citta*, that we call *mano*, that we call *viññāṇa*, by this the uninstructed people are not able to feel repelled, they are not able to show lack of passion for it or to be free from it. And why is this? For a long time, monks, it has been for the uninstructed that to which they cling, that which they call "mine," that which they wrongly conceive, thinking: that is mine; this I am; this is my spirit.[17]

This text ostensibly highlights the witless tendency of the average man to wrongly attach real existence and value to the mental faculties. However, it also points to an interesting parallelism of the psychological terms *citta*, *mano*, and *viññāṇa*. By listing each term separately the text indicates that they are to be regarded as having distinctive functions. Having gained some idea of what *viññāṇa* is and how craving pertains to it, *mano* and *citta* can be considered.

5. *Mano (Mana)*

This psychological term is often used to describe

the state of consciousness. Although it is an easier term to grasp than are *viññāṇa* and *citta*, it is still open to misunderstanding for two reasons.

First, because the term has a long history in Indian psychology, it is more open to preconceived interpretation. That *mano* has pre-Buddhist uses and connotations is certain. The term was freely applied both in the Upaniṣads and by the early Sāṃkhya philosophers. The question that arises, therefore, is whether the Buddha used *mano* in a manner consistent with one or more of the rival schools of his era? Although evidence throughout the Sutta Piṭaka points to a close relationship between early Buddhism and other contemporary schools of thought, it is difficult to show that a Buddhist psychological concept like *mano* is a notion established on a pre-Buddhist psychology. It is, though, apparent that the early Buddhist interpretation of *mano* bears some resemblance to the *manas* of the Upaniṣads and Sāṃkhya although it is also importantly different in certain respects.

In the Upaniṣads, *manas* is conceived not only as one of the sense organs,[18] but the person consisting of *manas* is said to be the supreme reality.[19] It is possible that the Upaniṣads regarded the sense organs as being material and subject to decay, while mind was more than just a sense organ in that it was immaterial, indestructible, immortal. But in Sāṃkhya, with its carefully defined dualism between eternal spirit (*puruṣa*) and impermanent matter (*prakṛti*), *manas* stands only in the latter category. Thomas points out that for them "not only the five senses but also the group to which mind belongs, stands on the material (*prakṛti*) side of nature."[20]

The early Buddhist use of *mano* lies somewhere between these two standpoints. On the one hand the *mano* of the Sutta Piṭaka, like the *manas* of the Sāṃkhya, is not considered to be eternal. On the other, like the *manas* of the Upaniṣads, Buddhist *mano* is not simply material. As a state of being it is more than this, with intellectual and conative properties which give it an ideational function of its own. The question is a complex one, but it is sufficiently evident that the Buddhist connotation of *mano*, though having roots in psychological terminology common to ancient India, is still unique. To avoid misunderstanding it is well to look beyond the history and use of the term in rival schools to the evidence of the Sutta Piṭaka to see the import of this concept in the Buddhist psychology of consciousness.

Second, misunderstanding also arises from an inadequate appreciation of the role of *mano* as a "sixth sense" in Buddhism. *Mano* is frequently referred to as "the grey matter of the brain," without any further elaboration.[21] Notwithstanding, this gives a completely distorted picture of what *mano* does in fact represent. We must therefore clear aside erroneous interpretations, and secure a textually sound definition of the early Buddhist meaning of *mano*. But in doing this, *mano* also has to be exhibited in its relation to craving.

The *mano* of the Sutta Piṭaka is to be understood as one of the physical senses. Because Buddhism does not firmly discriminate the external from the internal world, the ideations (*dhammā*) of *mano* were considered to be "real" like the physical stimuli of the other senses: form (*rūpa*) is the stimulus of eye (*cakkhu*); sound (*sadda*) is the stimulus of ear (*sota*); smell (*gandha*), that of nose (*ghāna*); taste (*rasa*), that of tongue (*jivhā*); touch or tangibility (*phoṭṭhabba*), that of body (*kāya*). Likewise, *mano* is a sense—but an internal sense which perceives ideas (*dhammasaññā*). Understood in this way, it is sometimes referred to as the sixth organ of perception. But although *mano* is one of the senses, it must be emphasized that, in a special way, it is more than this; *mano* is the "integrator" or matrix of the other senses: "Of the five senses, different in range, different in field, not reacting to the field and range of each other, *mano* is the refuge, and *mano* resonates to their field and range."[22]

A second function concerns the nature of the responsiveness or resonance attributed to it. M.3.216 outlines the way *mano* experiences feeling or discriminates (*upavicarati*) the quality of each sensory perception as it originates in any of the senses:

> When it is said "eighteen ranges (applications) of *mano* are to be known," in reference to what grounds is it said? Having seen a material form with the eye, one experiences the form as giving rise to pleasure (*somanassaṭṭhānīyaṃ*), experiences the form as giving rise to discomfort, experiences the form as giving rise to indifferent feeling. Having heard a sound with the ear, having smelt a smell with the nose...having tasted a flavour with the tongue...having felt a touch with the body...having become conscious of an ideation (*dhammaṃ*) with *mano*, because of that ideation one experiences (a mental state) giving rise to pleasure... discomfort or indifference. In this way there are six ranges for pleasure, six ranges for discomfort, six ranges for indifference. When it is said, "eighteen ranges of *mano* are to be known," it is said in reference to this.

Mano has a third function as a bridge between the senses and consciousness:

> Your reverence, if the ear that is internal is intact...the nose that is internal is intact...the tongue that is internal is intact...the body that is internal is intact... the mind that is internal is intact, but external mental objects do not come within its range, then there is no appearance of the appropriate section of consciousness. But when, your reverence, the mind that is internal (*ajjhattiko...mano*) is intact and external mental objects come within its range and there is appropriate impact, then there is thus an appearance of the appropriate section of consciousness (*viññāṇabhāgassa pātubhavo hoti*). M.1.191

To this point the description of *mano* is partly physiological (as one of the sense organs) and partly ideational (as integrator of the perceptual process). It is in its ideational capacity that *mano* assumes its real power in Buddhist epistemology. Not only does it have feeling and emotion; the Sutta Piṭaka indicates also that *mano* "thinks" (*manovitakkā*, S.1.207), has "imagination" ("I have gone into detachment in the forest, but my *mano* goes astray outside"—"*Vivekakāmo si vanaṃ paviṭṭho, atha te mano niccharati bahiddhā.*" S.1.197), and "memory" ("because I am old and feeble, my body does not go there, but in my intentions (*saṃkappa*) I always go there, for my *mano* is joined to his"—"*Jiṇṇassa me dubbalathāmakassa ten'eva kāyo na paleti tattha, saṃkappayattāya vajāmi niccaṃ, mano hi me...tena yutto.*" Sn.1144).[23]

Mano, it is clear, does far more than merely assemble and pass along sense impressions. Its active, dynamic role is nowhere more evident than in its association with intention and action, both good and bad. It is in this capacity that *mano*'s relation to craving and its related forces is most clearly shown.

6. *Mano* and Craving

There is a close relationship between craving and the "four foods." One of those "foods" is *manosañcetanā*, a compound term best translated as "mental volition," "will," or "purposiveness." The strategic text S.2.98 indicates that *mano* can be affected by *taṇhā*, and that the results of this exposure to craving are realized in willing and purposiveness.

This being so, *mano* plays an important role in the Buddhist "theology of intention." This is brought out firmly in S.2.97, M.1.256, D.3.288, and in other texts, such as Dhm. 233: "Let one be mindful (watchful) of *mano* irritation. Let him practise restraint of *mano*. Having abandoned the 'sins' of *mano* (*manoduccaritaṃ*), let him practise virtue with his mind." Such passages emphasize one of the most crucial issues in Buddhism. It is the intention, the purposiveness, which lies behind *mano*, that is so strategic. A further corollary of this "theology" declares that acts of body and speech are less significant than the thought which lies behind them. This teaching is in many ways the raison d'être of the Vināya Piṭaka. It is also carefully developed in the Sutta Piṭaka, as, for instance, in M.1.373:

> Dighatapassin the Jain spoke thus to the Blessed One: "But, friend Gotama, how many kinds of wrong (*daṇḍāni*) do you lay down for the performance of an evil deed (*kiriyāya pāpassa kammassa*) for the rolling on (*pavattiyā*) of an evil deed?"
> "Tapassin, it is not the custom of a Tathāgata to lay down 'wrong, wrong.' Rather, Tapassin, it is the custom for a Tathāgata to lay down 'deed, deed' (*kammaṃ*)."
> "But how many kinds of deeds do you lay down, friend Gotama, for the performance of an evil deed, for the rolling on of an evil deed?"
> "Tapassin, I lay down three kinds of deeds for the effecting of an evil deed, the deeds of body, speech, and *mano*."
> "But, friend Gotama, is deed of body one thing, deed of speech another, deed of *mano* another?"
> "Tapassin, deed of body is one thing, deed of speech another, deed of *mano* another."
> "But friend Gotama, of these three deeds thus separated, thus particularized, which deed do you lay down as the more blameable in the effecting of an evil deed, the rolling on of an evil deed?"
> "Tapassin, of these three deeds thus separated, thus particularized, I lay down that deed of *mano* as the more blameable in the effecting of an evil deed, in the rolling on of an evil deed; deed of body is not like it, deed of speech is not like it."
> "Did you say 'deed of *mano*,' friend Gotama?"
> "I say 'deed of *mano*,' Tapassin."

Mano's relation to bad traits, craving, and unskilled states of mind (*akusalā dhammā*, M.3.49) further indicates its moral accountability. At the same time, the texts point out that, like *citta* and *viññāṇa*, *mano* may be cultivated and developed in thoughtfulness (Dhm. 233) and in meditation. Elsewhere (Dhm. 96) *mano* is referred to as calmed (*santā*), as if released from the commotions of craving. By calming *mano*, speech and deeds become less agitated, tranquillity is achieved, and, with tranquility, freedom (*vimutti*) from mental irritants: "His *mano* is calm, calm his word as well as deed, when he has obtained freedom through true knowledge and has become tranquil." This does not, however, mean that *mano* can experience nirvāṇa, as *citta* does; or that it can "evolve" into another life, as *viññāṇa* does. The changing, transitory state of *mano* is never lost sight of, and at death it meets the same end as the other senses:

> Dependent upon *mano* and mental states, consciousness of the sixth sense (*manoviññāṇam*) arises. *Mano* is impermanent, changing, becoming something different (*aniccaṃ vipariṇāmi aññathābhāvi*). The mental states are impermanent, changing, becoming something different.
> S.4.69

Summing up: the basic psychological operations of *mano* are seen in its co-ordinating role as it receives impressions from the other senses. It is instrumental in the perceptive, feeling, and thinking (*manovitakka*, *manosankhāra*) processes. Its "theological" significance, however, lies in the fact that it is an active agency of will (*manosañcetanā*), which makes it able to govern the disposition and quality of moral, or immoral, acts. In this capacity, we can best observe its inseparable relation to craving.

7. *Citta*

Citta is the most complex psychological term in Buddhism, made more so by the great attention given to it in the Abhidhamma Piṭaka.[24] Even in the Sutta Piṭaka *citta* is difficult to grasp, and it is easy to get lost in the tangle of definitions. It is more appropriate to approach it by way of certain questions that arise from an important text. The clearest is M.3.32:

> Monks, the account of the monk in whom the cankers are destroyed, who has lived the life and done what has to be done, laid down the burden, attained his own welfare, in whom the fetters of becoming are destroyed and who is freed by right knowledge, would be in accordance with *dhamma* were he to say: Your reverences, whatever is desire, whatever is attachment, whatever is delight, whatever is craving for eye, material shape, visual consciousness (*cakkhuviññāṇe*) and for things cognisable through visual consciousness—by the destruction of these things, by stopping and giving up grasping after these things, which are mental dogmas, biases, and tendencies, I comprehend that my mind (*cittaṃ*) is freed. Your reverences, so it is with the ear, sounds, auditory consciousness ...the nose, smells, olfactory consciousness...the tongue, tastes, gustatory consciousness...the body, tactile objects, bodily consciousness...the mind, mental states, mental consciousness, with mental states cognisable through mental consciousness (*manoviññāṇaviññātabbesu*). So, your reverences, as I know thus, and see thus in respect of these six internal sense fields, I can say that my mind is freed from the cankers with no grasping remaining.

For two reasons, this passage takes us a long way in our understanding of *citta*. One, the text makes a fundamental distinction between *viññāṇa* and *citta*. *Viññāṇa* is described in terms of the rapidly changing surface consciousness represented by the six senses (*saḷāyatana*). Two, *citta* does not have this fractured appearance. It is involved with the senses only if it is under the sway of craving, and it seems to have a deeper background than *viññāṇa*, as if it were an experiential core of personality. This reading of the term *citta* does not mean that Buddhists regard it as the self. But the text does point out that through craving (*taṇhā*) and the related synonyms of *chanda*, *rāga*, *upādāna*, and *anusaya*, it is bound to the senses, and that in this way it is a kind of focus for what Johansson calls "emotions, desires and moral defilements."[25]

There is a great deal of evidence to support the definition of *citta* as a mental factor burdened with morally objectionable emotions and selfish needs. There is also equal evidence to demonstrate how *citta* can be developed and trained, and how it alone of all psychological factors can be said to experience nirvāṇa. The study of these two aspects of *citta*, the natural or "untrained" *citta* of the average individual and the "trained" *citta* of the liberated one, will tell us something about how craving arises, how it operates in this vital "centre of emotions," and how it can be neutralized.

8. The Untrained *Citta* and Craving

The untrained *citta* has many attributes. The texts indicate that, like *mano* and *viññāṇa*, *citta* is not a concrete, physical affair, but is incorporeal (*asarīra*, Dhm. 37); and, although it is sometimes said to depend on sensory stimulation (*phassāyatana* - S.4.125), it is even more closely involved with perception (*saññā*, S.4.293) and feelings (*vedanā*; i.e., "perception and feeling are mental processes dependent on *citta*. Thus perception and feeling are called the activity of the *citta*"—"*saññā ca vedanā ca cetasikā ete dhammā cittapaṭibaddhā, tasmā saññā ca vedanā ca cittasankhāro ti*"). This does not mean that *citta* is the "center" of perception, a function more in keeping with *mano*. *Citta* remains, however, receptive and susceptible to the influences of perception. Aside from its sensitivity to perception, the natural *citta* also has memory (M.1.22, D.1.81) and intellectual faculties ("understand with *citta*—"*cittena*...*ñassati*," A.1.9).

These aspects receive little attention in the Sutta Piṭaka compared to what it has to say about the emotional nature of the untrained *citta*. But one must distinguish between feelings (*vedanā*—be they pleasant or unpleasant) and the states of affectivity or "lack of balance" which can properly be called emotion, represented by such attributes as trembling and nervousness (*paritassanā*, S.3.16), carnal obsession (*kāmāsava*, D.1.84), anger (*padosa*, D.1.71; *savera*, D.1.247), apathy (*līna*, S.5.112), and mental disturbance or imbalance (*uddhata*, S.5.112).[26] In the last chapter it was pointed out how the term emotion does not sufficiently describe the epistemological function of feeling (*vedanā*). Emotion is deeper than feeling. In the case of the untrained *citta* emotion is associated with gross desires and bad moral traits, sometimes with *taṇhā* (Dhm. 154), though more often with *rāga* (passion or desire, S.1.185), the *āsavā* (cankers, D.1.84), *lobha* (greed, M.1.36), and the *upakkilesā* (general depravity, the so-called "moral defilements"). M.1.36 points out:

> And what, monks, are the moral defilements (*upakkilesā*) of *citta*? Greed and covetousness is a defilement, malevolence...anger...malice ...hypocrisy...spite...envy... stinginess...deceit...treachery ...obstinacy...impetuousness ...arrogance...pride...conceit ...indolence is a defilement of *citta*.

Having these unattractive features, the untrained *citta* is also said to be difficult to manage (*dūrakkha*, Dhm. 33) and to be instumental in allowing "unguarded" (*arakkhitaṃ* or *arakkhiya*) bodily (*kāyakamma*) and mental (*manokamma*) actions (A.1.261).

What does this tell us about *citta's* involvement with craving? One must notice how open the untrained *citta* is to assault by the senses and their craving for satisfaction. Even when the actual noun *taṇhā* is not used in direct conjunction with *citta*, it is enough to point out, as in M.3.32 above, that several other synonyms for craving (i.e., *chanda*, *rāga*, *upādāna*, *anusaya*) are used with *citta*. Johansson calls them the "adhesive tape of *taṇhā*"[27] which bind *citta* to the consciousness (*viññāṇa*) of the five senses (i.e., eye consciousness, ear consciousness, etc.), and thence to their objects and physical stimuli. The untrained *citta* is, therefore, very much under the influence of craving, and its liberation depends first and foremost on ridding itself of this "tape" which secures it to the world of consciousness and thence *saṃsāra*.

Clearly, the untrained *citta* cannot escape rebirth. The texts are basically consistent about this and point out that, like consciousness (*viññāṇa*), desire for rebirth seems to affect *citta*:

> Monks, I will teach you what it means to hope for "uprising" (after death) (*saṃkhāruppatiṃ*). Herein, a monk is endowed with faith, moral habit, learning, renunciation, wisdom. It occurs to him: "O that at the breaking up of the body after dying I might arise in companionship with the nobles. He fixes his *citta* on this, he resolves his *citta* on this, he develops his *citta* for this. These aspirations and "abidings" (*vihāro*) contribute to rebirth there. This, monks, is the way, this is the course that contributes to uprising there.
> M.3.99

Viññāṇa and *citta* are both subject to this cycle of rebirth, a fact that invites the question: Is there in rebirth any real difference between the two factors? Johansson points out that in the case of ordinary rebirth, when both *viññāṇa* and *citta* are said to undergo the same process, "we may assume a simple identification" between the two.[28] For the trained *citta* this is not so: its function is set apart from the grosser elements, one that is soteriologically very important.

9. The Trained *Citta*

A trained *citta* is controlled, not one that would "wander formerly as it liked, as it desired, as it pleased" ("*acārī cāritam yenicchakaṃ yatthakāmaṃ yathāsukham*" Dhm. 326). When free from deleterious desires it is not receptive to emotion. D.2.81 points out that: "*Citta*, when thoroughly developed through wisdom, is set free from the cankers, that is to say, the cankers of sensuality...wrong views and ignorance" —"*Paññā paribhāvitaṃ cittaṃ sammad eva āsavehi vimuccati seyyathīdaṃ kāmāsavā...diṭṭhāsavā avijjāsava ti.*" It is further described in this state as serene (*samāhita*, D.1.76), restrained (*saṃvuta*, A.1.7), and calm (*vūpasanta*, D.1.71), able to purge itself from "unskilled" (*akusala*) moral habits, to change its nature from bad traits to good ones: "that *citta* which is free from desire, free from anger, and free from illusion...originating from this are the wholesome moral habits"—" *yaṃ cittaṃ vītarāgaṃ vītadosaṃ vītamohaṃ, itosamuṭṭhānā kusalasīlā*" (M.2.27). This passage is interesting because it makes it plain that *citta* can bring to control a number of unwholesome traits.

The question of the control and training of *citta* is strategic to Buddhist meditational practice. As one of the four applications of mindfulness (*cāttaro satipaṭṭhānā*—contemplation of body, feeling, mind objects, and *citta*), the devotee strives to understand it under every condition, whether it is full of hate or greed, developed, concentrated, liberated, or not. The result of *citta* contemplation is to gain control over the experiential field. A.3.337 stresses this: "if objects cognizable by the eye come very strongly into the range of vision of a monk with wholly freed *citta*, they do not obsess his *citta*, and his *citta* is untroubled (*amissīkatam ev'assa cittaṃ hoti*), firm, having won to composure (*ṭhitaṃ ānejjappattaṃ*); and he watches it depart."

Citta, like consciousness (*viññāṇa*), also experiences the levels of awareness in meditation identified as the *jhānā*. The same can be said of *ceto*, also a derivative of the root *cit*. This point is important because in instances where the noun *ceto* appears it should be interpreted as being synonymous with *citta*.[29] But unlike *viññāṇa* at the ninth and final *jhāna*, *citta* alone can realize the ultimate experience of freedom from the cankers (*āsavā*). It is *citta* that experiences the calming of the Five Grasping Groups, the stilling of consciousness; it is *citta* that can become steady (*ṭhita*), calm (*vūpasanta*), that experiences nirvāṇa:

> Monks, if one's *citta* is not attached to the element of form (*rūpadhātuyā*) (as well as feeling, perception, activities, consciousness) and is released from the cankers without any conditions (*āsavehi vimuttatā ṭhitam*), then by its release it is steadfast; by its steadfastness it is content; being content it does not become excited; free from excitement, it attains nirvāṇa itself. S.3.45

A striking feature of the term *citta* is the range of its emotional, moral, and dispositional aspects. Like the term *viññāṇa*, *citta* refers to a reality which is dynamic and changing, open to sensory impression, capable of being manipulated by craving, thus involved in the process of rebirth. And yet, in its trained state, *citta* functions apart from the Five Groups (which, of course, include *viññāṇa*), or from any of the factors of the Series of Dependencies for that matter. No single word translates it adequately.[30] Attempts to make such terms as personality or ego serve in this capacity are open to controversy, if only because they carry contemporary semantic, philosophical, or theological connotations. Nevertheless *citta* does have some identification with what contemporary psychologists call the ego, at least in the Freudian sense which regards it as the center of perceptual and cognitive activity, open both to conscious and unconscious needs and to conduct.[31] It best expresses the constitution, quality, and character of the personality. In this it has no permanent value, being subject to the doctrine of non-self, like all Buddhist psychological concepts. But it is fair to say that, of these concepts, *citta* is rather more like an "entity" (as apart from process) of mind and personality than the others. This is a major reason why it receives careful attention in both the Sutta and Abhidhamma Piṭakas. At the same time, because of its close involvement with craving, and because it is regarded as the fundamental "problem-child" of the monk in particular, *citta* not unexpectedly undergoes examination in the Sutta Piṭaka as a crucial part of the soteriological problem of craving.

So far the principal components of the Buddhist psychology of consciousness have been described. Its wider applicability has been left to the next chapter. But some remarks concluding the present section will help us see *viññāṇa*, *citta*, and *mano* as a whole, as descriptive of a unit of consciousness rather than as a fractured cluster of unrelated mental phenomena.[32]

Simplified summaries of the Buddhist psychological account are difficult. Popular expositions rely upon diagrams which mean to show the numerous, complex psychological factors in relation to each other. These are usually insufficient and perhaps misleading because they tend to establish rigid boundaries around mental phenomena and translate them into optical images. If one must attempt to visualize such concepts as *viññāṇa*, *citta*, and *mano*, it has to be remembered that their functions often overlap. This makes conceptual categorical discrimination hazardous. Nonetheless, some scheme of relation might be usefully attempted.

In a cautious way, a metaphoric canvas or "picture" could start with the physical stimulations of form, sound, smell, taste, and touch. They might be shown to be related to consciousness as both *viññāṇa* and *mano*. As impressions on *viññāṇa*, the physical stimuli provoke the "*viññāṇa* process," a rapidly fluctuating surface consciousness which continues throughout the waking hours. As impressions on *mano*, the physical stimuli first initiate the three basic feelings of ease, pain, and indifference (*somanassa, domanassa, upekkhā*); subsequently, they affect a state of willing or intention (*sañcetanā*). *Mano* appears as a somewhat deeper form of consciousness than *viññāṇa*. The aggregate of this structure can then be depicted as bound to *citta* through craving and its related synonyms (as *chanda, rāga, upādāna, anusaya*, M.3.32), because these forces are the bridge by which the cognitive and ideational world of *viññāṇa* and *mano* cross over into *citta*.

In the sketch, *citta* is also affected by perception. Yet much of its function is set apart from the perceptual processes, for *citta* has personality factors not present in *viññāṇa* and *mano*. These personality factors point to its potential for moral energy and purpose, which are to be exhibited by its role in meditation. Here alone of all the concepts of consciousness *citta* can eradicate the cankers (the *āsavā* of sensual desire, desire for life, ignorance, and opinions).

We see that our "picture" of *citta* in many ways embraces the functions of *viññāṇa* and *mano* in that both surface consciousness and ideation are also to be included in the *citta* factor. Yet because of its more profound response to conscious stimuli, *citta* is to be regarded as the heart of personality, the deep background of purposiveness and emotion. And this is not all: the evidence shows that *citta* includes more than one layer of consciousness—not just the surface consciousness of *viññāṇa*, or the integrating, emotive consciousness of *mano*. In states of trance or sleep *viññāṇa* and *mano* are largely if not completely neutralized. But *citta* can still know (*jānāti*, M.1.523), can still reflect and contemplate (*paccavekkhana*).

To complete the canvas we must bring out the way in which craving operates throughout the mental structure as its major "adhesive." Craving infects each of the components we have considered. Starting with its genesis in the primitive urgings incited by perception, craving becomes increasingly complex, affecting not only the direction of the "*viññāṇa* process" but also the ideational response of *mano* to sense impressions, dictating mental attitude and the physical response of conduct. Its most potent and damaging consequence, however, lies in its effect on the individual will. To some extent *viññāṇa*, *citta*, and *mano* are agencies of willing, since they contribute to purposiveness, direction, and intention. Craving (*taṇhā*) conditions the will at each stage of consciousness, and is even able to cripple the only faculty (*citta*) which has potential to neutralize it.

The psychological or spiritual import of this schema cannot be underestimated, but of still greater importance is the religious dimension which it brings forward. The etiology of craving as part of the conscious process has now been reviewed and the psychological basis for the Buddhist "theology of intention" established. It is this "theology of intention," to coin a phrase, which underlies craving's critical position as the central emphasis in Buddhist soteriology. This will become increasingly evident in the next chapter, when we come to discuss craving and meditation. For the present, there remains only one major responsibility, to investigate the evidence which reveals a remarkably perceptive psychology of the unconscious.

10. The Unconscious and *Taṇhā*

In an article on early Buddhist psychology written in 1924, J. T. Sun observed: "The Buddhist knows that by living a life governed by conscious wisdom and not by unconscious craving there will result a personality but little affected by sorrow."[33] Perhaps without full awareness, Sun was the first modern scholar to touch upon an issue of great importance, the matter of the unconscious in Buddhism. To come at this topic in a methodical way, we need first to review what scholarship has contributed to this subject, define the limitations of these attainments, and then set about to examine for ourselves the evidence of the Sutta Piṭaka. The inquiry will concentrate on the concept of *sankhāra*, one of the most complex and vital terms in Buddhist psychology. Other concepts, such as the latent dispositions (*anusayā*, *akusala mūlā*) and the cankers (*āsavā*), all indicate an unconscious state. As in our study of the Buddhist understanding of consciousness, we aim for a total psychological picture. Once this has been worked out, a clearer idea about the relationship between unconscious states, consciousness, and craving should be evident.

11. Previous Scholarship

The idea of unconscious activity has only recently become a topic of interest to Buddhist students of the Pāli scriptures.[34] Apart from J. T. Sun (whose essay provides us only with general observations but no direct textual references), a mere handful of scholars have made serious attempts to investigate the issue as it appears in the Sutta Piṭaka. Of these, W. F. Jayasuriya, K. N. Jayatilleke, and M. W. P. de Silva are notable, particularly de Silva, whose arguments are the most carefully and extensively developed. Jayatilleke makes no mention of a Buddhist concept of the unconscious in his principal work, Early Buddhist Theory of Knowledge (1963), but in several other essays he refers to the likelihood of such a perspective in the Sutta Piṭaka. Thus, in "Buddhism and the Scientific Revolution" he writes:

> In psychology we find early Buddhism regarding man as a psychophysical unit whose "psyche" is not a changeless soul but a dynamic continuum composed of a conscious mind as well as an unconscious in which is stored the residue of emotionally charged memories going back to childhood as well as into past lives.[35]

In another essay, "Some Problems of Translation and Interpretation,"[36] Jayatilleke investigates the exegesis of the noun *sankhāra* and points out that it must have a conative meaning, with an unconscious as well as conscious dimension. But Jayatilleke's study does not go far enough. There is, for instance, no mention of the role of the latent tendencies (*anusayā*) or roots (*mūlā*) in the unconscious. To some extent this omission is remedied by Jayasuriya, who suggests that the latent tendencies are like the psychoanalytic notion of the unconscious.[37]

The most compelling study of a Buddhist theory of the unconscious is offered by M. W. Padmasiri de Silva,[38] who has made Buddhist psychology intelligible and important to contemporary Western readers. He, like Rune Johansson, seeks to place Buddhist psychology and language within a Western setting, specifically by use of Western psychological terminology to characterize Buddhist ideas. We are, for instance, rightly cautioned to use a word such as "unconscious" with consistency, and to avoid the use of the term "subconscious" to describe those aspects of mental activity of which we are not fully conscious. The term subconscious is largely undefined in use and is therefore open to misleading interpretations.

Perhaps de Silva's most profound contribution is his pioneering work in seeing similarities between modern Western psychological concepts and those of the Buddha. But for present purposes, which are not by intention specifically comparative, de Silva can be helpful in the way he has come to grips with the latent tendencies, roots, and cankers. He argues, for instance, that in many ways these factors are best understood as unconscious forces, and that the Buddhist notion of the unconscious can be made more intelligible in the light of the Freudian theory of the unconscious. The same can be said for de Silva's comparative analysis of the theory of motivation in Freud and Buddhism, where like Jayatilleke[39] he carefully unfolds an argument which provides interesting parallels between the Freudian instincts of ego, libido, and the death instinct with one of the traditional three-fold classifications of craving—craving for sensuality (*kāmataṇhā*), for life (*bhavataṇhā*), and for the power of destruction (*vibhavataṇhā*) (S.5.421). A student of Buddhism might argue that the Freudian instincts, residing as they do for the most part in the id, cannot be said to be conscious, whereas craving (*taṇhā*) in the Series of Dependencies (*paṭiccasamuppāda*) is said to be part of a stream of consciousness (*viññāṇa-sotaṃ*). De Silva must be aware of this, and surely he would agree that the unconscious in Freud's early work may have been identified only with the id, but that his mature doctrine maintained that all mental activity (excluding, of course, consciousness in the narrow sense of self-consciousness-ness) may be unconscious. A final reference should be made to de Silva's interest in Buddhism as a system of psychological "therapy." Here again there are interesting parallels with Western examples, although ultimately, de Silva argues, Buddhist "therapy" has to be appreciated in the light of a religious perspective if it is not to be misunderstood. We owe much to the exploratory and analytical research of de Silva, and we profit from his observation when we deal with a good many passages from the Sutta Piṭaka.

Apart from the foregoing, modern scholarship in Buddhist psychology has not been particularly fruitful in developing a case for an account of the unconscious in the Sutta Piṭaka. Even Johansson, whose otherwise informative study on the mind cannot be surpassed for comprehensiveness, does not venture into this region except for a couple of references to Jayatilleke's findings.

What evidence is there for a notion of the unconscious in the texts? A good place to start is with the crucial term *sankhāra*.

12. *Sankhāra*

Although in the present context the intention is to develop the idea of the unconscious in the semantics of the term *sankhāra*, this will be more meaningful if it is seen in its relation to the larger conative context of *sankhāra*. The method of this section suggests that it first be demonstrated why *sankhāra* should be regarded principally as a conative term, and second, that in this capacity one of its unique aspects expresses certain conative dispositions which are unconscious.

In its opening comments on the word *sankhāra*, the Pāli Text Society dictionary sums up the predicament Western translators face in coming to grips with this term. It remarks that:

> *Sankhāra* is one of the most difficult terms in Buddhist metaphysics, in which the blending of the subjective—objective view of the world and of happening, peculiar to the East, is so complete that it is almost impossible for Occidental terminology to get at the root of its meaning in a translation. We can only convey an idea of its import by representing several sides of its application without attempting to give a "word" as a definite translation.

One reaction to this dilemma is to turn to the etymology of the word in the hope of seeking a basic meaning. As we have indicated, the basis of the term is in the original Sanskrit verb *kṛ*, which is by itself very complex.[40] It can be demonstrated that this root refers on the one hand to something that is put together, as a compound (*sankhata*) or aggregate ("all component things are impermanent"—"*aniccā sabbe sankhārā*," S.1.200). On the other hand, the root *kṛ* can also be shown to lie behind the Sanskrit noun *kratu*, which has a distinctly conative meaning.[41]

The root structure of *sankhāra* indicates, therefore, two possible meanings. In the Sutta Piṭaka there is evidence that occasionally *sankhāra* is used to specify "aggregate," "component things," "syntheses," or "composition" (S.1.200, 3.86; Thera. 5.10). That *sankhāra* can refer to phenomenal existence is true enough, and it is often found translated as such. But in the majority of references to *sankhāra* in the Sutta Piṭaka a more likely interpretation reveals psychological and conative meanings. *Sankhāra* is therefore very much a "dynamic" term. What kind of evidence strengthens this claim?

13. *Sankhāra* as Volition

Not infrequently *sankhāra* is used synonymously with other conative Pāli terms. Thus in A.1.32 we read:

> Monks, in a man of wrong view (*micchādiṭṭhikassa*) all deeds of body done according to that view, all deeds of speech...of thought...of volition (*cetanā*), aspiration (*patthanā*), mental resolve (*paṇidhi*), and willing (*sankhārā*); all such things contribute to the unpleasant, the distasteful, the repulsive, the unprofitable, in short, to painfulness.

Here as elsewhere (S.3.60) the central notion of willing is identified with *sankhāra*. In A.1.32 *sankhāra* is used in the sense of effecting a course of action leading to "dark results" now and to rebirth at death, an import found in other passages as well, notably A.1.122 and M.1.389:

> And what, Punna, is the deed that is dark with dark results? Here, Punna, someone effects a harmful or malevolent (*sabyābajjhaṃ*) activity of the body (*kāyasankhāraṃ*), of speech, of the mind. He, having effected an activity of the body that is harmful, arises in a world that is harmful.

Elsewhere *sankhāra* assumes the sense of making a calculated choice between courses of action, as in D.3.217 (three *sankhārā*: those effecting meritorious, demeritorious and neutral actions—*tayo sankhārā: puññābhisankhāro, apuññābhisankhāro, āneñjābhisankhāro*), M.1.391 and A.2.230:

> Monks, I have come to understand, realize, and know these four deeds. What four? There is the dark deed with a dark result, a bright (*sukkaṃ*) deed with a bright result; a deed that is both dark and bright, with a dark and bright result; and the deed that is neither dark nor bright, with a result neither dark nor white, which being itself a deed contributes to the dissolution (*saṃvattati*) of deeds. And of what sort is the deed that is dark with a dark result? In this case ...a certain one effects willed bodily action (likewise action of thought

> and speech) that is harmful (*savyāpajjhaṃ kāyasankhāraṃ abhisankharoti*). And what sort is the bright deed with the bright result? In this case, one effects willed bodily action that is not harmful.... And what sort is the deed that is both dark and bright, with a result that is both dark and bright? In this case, one effects willed bodily action that is joined with both harm and harmlessness. And of what sort is the deed that is neither dark nor bright, with a result that is similar, which, being itself a deed, contributes to the dissolution of deeds? In this case, monks, it is volition (*cetanā*) that abandons this dark deed with the dark result... bright deed with the bright result, deeds both dark and bright.

This passage points out how *sankhāra* describes consciously performed acts initiated by the conative attitude of the individual. But the text is important also for a different yet crucial reason. As in M.1.391, *sankhāra* is here used in conjunction with volition (*cetanā*)—only with this distinction, that in these passages *cetanā* is the volitional term used for that act of deliberation which does away with acts that are prone to rebirth. Does this mean that *sankhāra* is limited only to gross and detrimental willing, whereas *cetanā* refers to pure and refined willing? This sometimes seems to be the case, but it is not always so. For instance, as in S.3.60 above, in certain contexts *sankhāra* and *cetanā* are used synonymously. Even more telling is the relation which obtains between *cetanā* and "dark" deeds (*kammaṃ kaṇhaṃ*), for, as in A.3.415, *cetanā* is equated with deeds that are often "dark," and *cetanā* is not therefore always a pure kind of willing. As for *sankhāra* there are circumstances when it is used affirmatively, as in M.1.297, where the compound *abhisankhāra* is used to describe the preliminary act of volition needed to achieve certain stages of spiritual trance. The term *sankhāra* is not always a pejorative one. *Sankhāra* is not necessarily a disadvantageous conative force.

The use of the compound *abhisankhāra* just mentioned raised another important question. How does this term complement and further elucidate the conative role of *sankhāra*? Itself a complicated term, *abhisankhāra* is best looked at in the context of one or two critical passages, which will make its psychological function evident.

14. *Abhisankhāra* and the case of A.1.111

Like *sankhāra* the structural breakdown of *abhisankhāra* does little to help delineate the term's meaning. Apart from its usual translations as "karma" or "accumulations," it has been variously rendered as "substratum,"[42] "complexes,"[43] "planning,"[44] and "impulse."[45] Jayatilleke has made a bold interpretation of the term by translating it as "motive force."[46] This may be controversial, if only because motive is a widely misused and misunderstood word. But Jayatilleke's understanding of the word motive is consistent with common contemporary psychological usages of the word. In this regard de Silva has pointed out that motivation has a three-fold dimension reflecting stages in a cycle of, first, mental states that provoke behaviour; second, behaviour motivated by these states; and third, the goals of such behaviour. Behind motive, then, there is an "inner condition" that initiates and directs its movement towards a goal.[47] This is much the way Jayatilleke uses the term *abhisankhāra*, and from this perspective his translation of the word as "motive force" is justified.

There is an important Pāli text which indicates this sense of motive. It is set in an elaborate analogy known as the Parable of the Wheelwright (A.1.111). It is worth considering in some detail. An analogy is drawn between a chariot wheel and the wheel of life. The story centres on a certain king who asks his wheelwright to make a pair of chariot wheels and to be ready for battle six months hence. Six months less six days pass and the wheelwright has finished only one wheel. The king inquires whether the second wheel can be made in the short time that remains and he is told it can. Upon delivery of the wheels on the appointed day the king exclaims that, despite the difference in time it took to make each wheel, they appear to look alike and to have no structural differences. "But your honour," replies the wheelwright, "there is a difference. Let your honour look." The parable continues:

> This said, the wheelwright set rolling the wheel he had finished in six days. The wheel kept rolling so long as the impulse force (*abhisankhārassa gati*) that set it moving lasted. Then it circled around and around and fell to the ground. Then he set rolling the wheel which he had finished in six months less six days. It kept rolling so long as the impulse force that set it going lasted, and then stood still as if, you might think, it was stuck to the axle.

The reason for the discrepancy in the performance of each wheel is then revealed. The wheel made in six days had a crooked rim (*savaṅkā*), and the spokes and hub were defective, full of flaws (*sadosā sakasāvā*). The wheel made in six months less six days had none of these. "Owing to the even, faultless, flawless nature of the rim, spokes and hub," continued the wheelwright, "this wheel set rolling rolled on so long as the impulse force that set it moving lasted, then it stood still."

At this point the chariot wheels are compared to the individual in *saṃsāra*. The analogy between the physical impulse that moves the chariot wheels and the psychological orientation that motivates the individual in the "wheel of life" is striking. The Buddha instructs his listeners that he himself was the wheelwright in the parable, and just as he was expert (*kusalo*) in wood that was crooked and full of faults and flaws (*dāruvaṅkānaṃ dārudosānaṃ dārukasāvānaṃ*), so is he now an expert in the crooked ways, faults and flaws of body, speech, and mind. The one who remains crooked in motivation will fall away from the true law (*dhamma*), just like the wheel that was made in six days, and the one who is not crooked in motivation will stand firm in the *dhamma*, like the wheel made in six months less six days.

So far it has been argued that *sankhāra* and its related compounds (*abhisankhāra* and *abhisankharoti*) are volitional terms in both scope and usage. We have seen how *abhisankhara* indicates a momentum, a dynamic force that keeps the wheel rolling, and how this definition complements the dispositional nature of *sankhara*. Contributing as it does to meritorious, demeritorious, and "imperturbable" action, *sankhāra* is the effector of deeds (*kamma*) and therefore the principal factor of responsibility in the Series of Dependencies. But is it to be regarded as a conscious or unconscious responsibility, a conscious or unconscious volition? We must now turn to this important question in order to demonstrate that *sankhāra* reflects both conscious and unconscious willing.

15. *Sankhāra* Understood as Conscious and Unconscious Volition

Sankhāra has an obvious conscious conative dimension. This is seen in its relation to ignorance (*avijjā*), traditionally the first link in the Series of Dependencies. In the formula ("unconscious volitions are provoked by ignorance"—"*avijjā paccayā sankhārā*"), will and subsequent willed actions or deeds (*kamma*) are shown to be casually linked with one's level of attained truth. Because in Buddhism ignorance is usually associated with both conscious and unconscious indifference to the four Noble Truths, volition may emerge from the conscious as well as the unconscious disposition towards the truths. Thus ignorance prompts willed activities that can be morally unfavourable (*apuññābhisankhāra*, S.2.82), whereas a more enlighted response to the truths initiates morally superior willing.

Again, as seen in M.1.389 and A.2.230, *sankhāra* as

"seeking after ends" and as "making a choice" denotes a deliberate act of will, consciously carried out. Even in the sense of motivation *sankhāra* can be understood as a term of conscious willing.

Evidence for the claim that *sankhāra* also has an unconscious volitional dimension is harder to find. It is nonetheless present in several key texts. The first of these, A.1.170, cannot be considered an unusual or exceptional passage because it is the same as a similar text in D.3.104:

> Brahmin, what is the marvellous ability of mind reading (*ādesanāpaṭihāriyaṃ*, or "guessing other people's character")? In this case, a certain one can announce by means of a sign, this is your *mano*. Such and such is your *mano*, such and such your *citta*. And again, brahmin, perhaps he does so after hearing a voice from men or non-humans or spirits, or on judging some sound he has heard, an utterance intelligently made by one who is reasoning intelligently.... Then again, brahmin, in this case suppose a certain one does not announce by any of the signs, yet maybe, when he has attained a state of concentration which is free from cogitative and reflective thought (*avitakkaṃ avicāraṃ samādhiṃ*) can comprehend (*paricca*) thus: According to how the mental forces (*manosankhāre*) are disposed in the mind of this venerable one, he will think such a thought (*amun nāma vitakkaṃ*) now. A.1.170

Commenting on this strategic passage, Jayatilleke writes:

> As the subject is apparently not conscious of the presence of these *sankhārā* which subsequently determine or influence his processes of thought, they are presumably not present in his consciousness when they are perceived by the exercise of the telepathic powers of the other.... In this passage we therefore find perhaps the earliest historical mention of unconscious mental processes.[48]

Two other passages lend support to this account of the

unconscious. As mentioned, one of these is D.3.104f, where the Buddha teaches the four degrees of discernment (*dassana samāpatti*). The third and fourth degrees are described in terms of a divided stream of consciousness (*viññāṇa-sotaṃ*):

> Again, lord, he goes on after that to discern the unbroken flux of consciousness (*viññāṇa-sotaṃ*), established both in this world and in another world without a sharp distinction into two parts (*ubhayato abbocchinnaṃ*). This is the third degree of discernment. Again, lord, he goes on to discern the unbroken flux of consciousness as not established either in this world or in another world.

This crucial passage indicates that *viññāṇa*, which we have so far discussed only as a process of consciousness, also has a dimension in a "world beyond" (*para-loke patiṭṭhitañ*), something, Jayatilleke writes, that can be identified with the unconscious:

> As this is said to be so when the person is alive in this world it implies the presence of a part of the stream of consciousness of which the person is not aware though it nevertheless exists in a state of flux. And though there is no text to confirm this, the probability is that this part of the stream of consciousness consisted of these dynamic *sankhāras* which persisted in a state of flux in the unconscious influencing his subsequent behaviour.[49]

By its description as "*para-loke*" ("in a world beyond"), the dispositional nature of the unconscious may not be immediately apparent, but the probability that it consists of the *sankhārā* and the fact that it is in flux tend to reinforce the argument that we are still dealing with a dispositional definition of something unconscious. Furthermore, the relationship evident here between *sankhāra* and *viññāṇa* is justified in the light of the Series of Dependencies, where the formula "unconscious volitions provoke consciousness" (*sankhāra paccayā viññāṇam*") points out how the conative force of the *sankhārā* causally conditions consciousness, and that if some of these *sankhārā* are hidden from consciousness, they nonetheless still underlie that consciousness and condition its quality and attitude.

The fact that many of our bodily and mental functions have a conscious and unconscious volitional feature is also brought out in the terms "body, speech, and mind volitions" (*kāyasankhāra, vacīsankhāra,* and *cittasankhāra,* M.1.301). As in our citation from A.2.230, *kāyasankhāra* can be identified with conscious volitional acts executed by way of the body. But in M.1.301 it is also identified with breathing (*assāsapassāsā*), an action which describes a reflex or habit more often than not unwilled. Likewise, *vacīsankhāra, cittasankhāra,* and *manosankhāra* (A.2.158) have both conscious and unconscious volitional roles, as Jayatilleke correctly theorizes. He writes:

> All these *sankhāras* are further classified in another context where the use of the term *sankhāra* for "reflex actions" or unconscious habits of body, speech and mind is shown by the fact that we can operate a *sankhāra* (*sankhāraṃ abhisankharoti*) without being aware of it (*asampajāno*).[50]

It is important to point out, however, that these *sankhārā*, even if unconscious, can be brought before consciousness. This is not something the average individual (*puthujjana*) does. For him many of these "motives" are not correctly understood, or, for that matter, go completely unrecognized. They are impulsive in kind and so lack agent control. But for the one who is aware the discipline of meditation can enable him to make the unconscious conscious. He can, for example, will his breathing to stop, and even will to "let go" (*ossajjati*) of those "motive forces which sustain life" (Jayatilleke's translation of *āyusankhāra*), as, in D.2.106, the Buddha was said to have done. There will be more to say about this in the next chapter.

To sum up so far, there is evidence which points to a concept of the unconscious in the term *sankhāra*. We began by arguing that *sankhāra* is a volitional term denoting conscious willing (striving after ends and making a choice) as well as willed actions (*kamma*). This volitional meaning of *sankhāra* also applies to an unconscious dimension in the denotation of the term. Here, *sankhāra* reflects a dispositional construct of the unconscious and consists of both conative forces, which go largely unrecognized by the ordinary individual, and undeliberate reflex actions, such as breathing. We have also seen how the unconscious *sankhārā* are related to the arising of the "process of consciousness" (D.3.105) and how both *mano* (A.1.170, 2.158) and *citta* (M.1.301) are conditioned by these forces.

The picture of the unconscious is not yet complete, for the Sutta Piṭaka also makes reference to latent tendencies (*anusayā*) and dispositional roots (*mūlā*) which are largely unconscious. What do these tell us about the nature of the unconscious and about the etiology of craving?

16. Factors of the Unconscious: Dormant Tendencies, Dispositional Roots, and Cankers

Of the many lists of detrimental psychological features found in the Sutta Piṭaka,[51] three in particular are set down so as to suggest an unconscious component. These are the dormant tendencies or *anusayā*, the detrimental roots or *akusala mūlā*, and the cankers or *asāvā*.

We can begin with the dormant tendencies, where a case for unconscious dispositional factors is clearly indicated in the texts. The term *anusaya* has been variously translated as "latent bias," "latent tendency," or "unconscious disposition."[52] Dormant tendencies or inclinations are adequate translations of the word, and it is worth noting that it is always used in a pejorative sense. Traditionally there are seven of them, cited in S.5.60. Freely translated, this reads: "Seven dormant tendencies: the desire to satisfy the senses and sex (*kāmarāgānusaya*), anger or aggression (*paṭighānusaya*), superstitious beliefs adhered to (*diṭṭhānusaya*), doubt (*vicikicchānusaya*), personal pride and conceit (*mānānusaya*), egoistic impulses (*bhavarāgānusaya*), and ignorance (*avijjānusaya*). There are then two central aspects of the *anusayā*: on the one hand they are latent and therefore unconscious, and, on the other, they are dispositional. Frequently the *anusayā* are associated with the verb *anuseti* (*anu* + *seti* - to lie down, lie dormant), a verb which in turn reflects an unconscious state.[53]

A key text which emphasizes the close relation between the dormant tendencies and *anuseti* also points out how the dormant tendencies are present even in infancy, a source for potential painfulness in child and adult alike:

> If there was not a sense of "own body" (*sakkāyo*) for an innocent baby (*daharassa*) lying on his back, how could there arise for him the view of "own body"? A dormant tendency to the view of "own body" (*sakkāyadiṭṭhānusayo*) lies within him.... Likewise a dormant tendency for things (*dhammā*) leading to perplexity...for habits (*sīlā*)... sense pleasures (*kāmacchando*)... malevolence (*byāpado*)...." M.1.432

This passage brings out how unconscious harmful inclinations are passed on from life to life, doubtless through the process of karma. They appear to be deeper, almost instinctual forces, ready to excite craving. Behind conscious feelings lie the dormant tendencies, as M.1.303 illustrates:

> What tendency (*kiṃanusayo*) lies latent in pleasant feeling (*sukhāya... vedanāya...anuseti*), what tendency lies latent in painful feeling, what tendency lies latent in neutral feeling? Friend Visakha, a tendency to attachment lies latent in pleasant feeling, a tendency to anger or repugnance (*paṭighānusayo*) lies latent

> in painful feeling, a tendency to ignorance lies latent in neutral feeling.

In another important text (M.3.285) the dormant tendencies are shown as apart from the process of consciousness, yet still enter into the experiences that are generated by that process:

> Monks, visual consciousness arises because of eye and material shapes, the meeting of the three is sensory stimulus; an experience arises conditioned by sensory stimulation (*phassapaccayā*) that is pleasant or painful or neither painful nor pleasant. He, being stimulated by a pleasant feeling, delights, is happy, and persists in clinging to it; a tendency to passion is latent within him (*rāgānusayo anuseti*).

Having demonstrated the unconscious dispositional nature of the dormant tendencies, the issue of their relationship to craving (*taṇhā*) comes forward. One could establish a scheme of correspondence between the dormant tendencies and craving which views the former as a deeper background, an undercurrent that sustains conscious craving. Thus it could be argued that the dormant tendency of sensual lust (*kāmarāga*) forms the basis of sensual craving (*kāmataṇhā*), that the dormant tendency to cling to life (*bhavarāga*) is the basis for craving for life (*bhavataṇhā*), and that the dormant tendency of anger (*paṭigha*) is the basis for those aggressive tendencies which also make up craving for no-life (*vibhavataṇhā*).[54] As was evident in M.3.285 above, the dormant tendencies underlie the conscious process of which craving is a part. It can therefore be argued that the dormant tendencies contribute to the arising of consciously willed craving because they are the unconscious dispositional ground of each individual. Thus the baby in M.1.432 is said to have a feeling or "opinion" of selfhood; that is to say, he is the center of the world, so to speak, and that for anything to have meaning it must revolve around this self. Again, with the dormant tendencies of conceit (*māna*) and desire for life (*bhavarāga*), the stress falls upon the same egocentric pressure. The dormant tendency of conceit is the basis of the experience of pride and feeling of personal distinctiveness; the desire for life reminds us of the life force (*āyusankhāra*) and can be equated with the will to think "I am" (*asmimāna*, D.3.273), something to which most individuals obviously cling.[55]

Aside from the dormant tendencies, there are two other lists of detrimental traits which have an unconscious dimension. One of these is the unwholesome roots or the roots of immoral action (*akusala mūlā*).

17. The Unwholesome Roots

Traditionally the three roots (*mūlā*) of immoral action (unskilled states—*a* + *kusala*) are greed (*rāga*), corruption or hatred (*dosa*), and delusion (*moha*), although frequently the term *lobha* is used synonymously with *rāga*. It should be pointed out that there are as well three skillful or moral roots to counterbalance these, notably generosity (*arāga*), love (*adosa*), and knowledge (*amoha*).

The word root (*mūla*) is singularly graphic. By metaphor it points to a source for action and wholesome attitude. Some scholars identify the unwholesome roots with "fundamental evil motives," as Jayasuriya does when he points out that they are "unrecognized," and therefore the cause for evil actions and mental impurities.[56] This is consistent with the texts, where the *akusalā mūlā* are used to describe the arising of karma ("*kammānaṃ samudayāya*," A.1.264). Because karma is passed on from birth to birth it can be argued that the unwholesome roots are inherited unconscious dispositional forces that stand behind willed action. This seems to be suggested in A.1.263.

> Monks, were there karma performed by greed, born of greed, conditioned by greed, arising from greed—that karma is unwholesome (*akusalaṃ*), is blame-

> worthy (*sāvajjaṃ*), has painfulness as its fruit, leads to the further arising of more karma, does not lead to the cessation of karma. Monks, were there karma performed in hatred or in delusion, that karma is unwholesome.

This passage also emphasizes that karma is based on greed or desire (*rāga*), whether of the past, present, or even in the future. As one of the unwholesome roots, desire is the source of that attachment to which the infatuated mind (*sārāgo*) is fettered (*saññojanaṃ* or *saṃyojanam*) for the production of yet more desire, thus of more karma:

> Monks, there are these three conditions for the arising of karma. What three? For things which in the past were based on desire and excitement or wishing (*chanda-rāgaṭṭhānīye*)...in the future will be based on desire and excitement... in the present are based on desire and excitement. Now how is desire born for things which in the past, future, and present are based on desire and excitement? Things which in the past, future, or present are based on desire, one turns this over in his mind (*anuvitakketi anuvicāreti*). Thus turning things over in his mind, desire is born. Desire being born, he is fettered by those things. I call it a fetter, that mind full of infatuation. This is desire born for things which in the present are based on desire and attachment.

What now of the relation between the unwholesome roots and craving? It is important to point out that the roots are rather like some of the latent tendencies. Thus the root of greed (*ragamūla*) overlaps the inclination for sensual satisfaction (*kāmarāgānusaya*), the root of hatred (*dosamūla*) with the inclination for aggression (*paṭighānusaya*), and the root of delusion (*mohamūla*) with the inclination to ignorance (*avijjānusaya*). Furthermore, just as the dormant tendencies lie behind craving, for the same reasons it can be argued that the roots underlie and condition craving. Thus, for example, there is an evident correspondence between the root of greed and both sensual desire and the craving for life. The *mūlā* as "roots," then, are more than just a figure of speech. They play a crucial role in the etiology of craving (*taṇhā*).

18. The Cankers

The final group of harmful dispositions which underlie consciousness are the cankers (*āsavā*). This term has little currency in contemporary Buddhism. I found that lay people and even some monks in Sri Lanka, Burma, and Thailand rarely had an appreciation of its significance in the teachings (*dhamma*). Nevertheless its importance in the texts is apparent. Coming from the root *sru* (to ooze or flow), *āsava* has a specific function in Buddhist psychological terminology as "that which intoxicates the mind so that it cannot rise to higher things."[57] It is difficult to find an English equivalent for this word, but Horner's translation of canker[58] adequately conveys the sense of a psychological sore that festers corrosively. Johansson's "influxes" is less adequate.[59] In what are regarded as some of the older passages of the Sutta Piṭaka (M.1.55, A.1.165, S.4.256, Itv. 49), only three cankers are traditionally referred to (*kāmāsava, bhavāsava, avijjāsava*: the cankers of sensuality, of "becoming," and of ignorance). On occasion *diṭṭhāsava* (the canker of "views" or speculation) is added, as in D.2.81:

> The mind (*cittaṃ*) filled with
> wisdom (*paññā—paribhāvitaṃ*)
> is set free from the *āsavā*,
> that is to say from the cankers of
> sensuality, lust for life, specula-
> tion, and ignorance.

A significant feature of this passage is its reference to mind (*citta*). The cankers frequently appear in the context of this term, and the very fact that they seriously affect the mind and are the last detrimental dispositions to be removed before enlightenment points to their deeply entrenched position within the psyche. Only in the final stages of meditation does the devotee rid himself of these cankers:

> And presently, Ananda, passing wholly beyond the mental state of neither perception nor non-perception, I entered and abode in the cessation of perception and feeling, and I saw by wisdom that the cankers were destroyed. A.4.448

The cankers (*āsavā*) are evidently so established (and yet at the same time so common) that, as this passage and other texts point out, it takes a special kind of knowledge (*paññā*) to excise them. The ordinary person is unaware of this background; even those engaged in the first levels of meditation are unable to penetrate the depths of their dispositional nature sufficiently to discover the source of craving and so begin to eradicate it.

It can be claimed that the chief feature of the cankers is their power to thwart insight, particularly insight into the cause of painfulness. At least it is clear that the canker of ignorance is in many ways the most fundamental ("with the arising of cankers there is the arising of ignorance, with the cessation of cankers there is cessation of ignorance"—"*āsavasamudayā avijjāsamudayo āsavanirodhā avijjānirodho*," M.1.54). It is the basis of all harmful states of mind. No other factor is as impure (*malā malatram*, as in Dhm. 243: "But the superlative impurity, greater than all the others, is ignorance.").

It is important to point out that the ignorance specifically indicated by the canker of ignorance is want of the higher knowledge, the four Noble Truths. Not unexpectedly several texts stress the destruction of the cankers as coinciding with the realization of these Truths (D.2.98). As this and other passages indicate, rooting out the cankers is a vital component of the Buddhist way to awareness. One does not find the dormant tendencies or unwholesome roots directly mentioned in such a context.[60] It is also notable that the cankers are referred to many more times in the Sutta Piṭaka than the dormant tendencies or roots, confirming their critical importance in Buddhist soteriology. Their intransigent, powerful grip on the individual, shown by their presence at even the most profound level of meditation, indicates the extent of their influence on the personality (*citta*). In this way the cankers are even less readily brought to the realization and understanding of an enlightened consciousness than the latent tendencies or the unwholesome roots. They represent the deepest unconscious dispositional forces of the human pscyhe.

To sum up, accounts of the dormant tendencies, unwholesome roots, and cankers are found in the Pāli scriptures, and represented as groups of harmful dispositions or traits which are unconscious. Although several of the traits overlap and are found in all three lists, each group is regarded as having a distinct function which sets it apart. Thus, only the dormant tendencies are referred to directly as being "*anuseti*" or latent dispositions. The unwholesome roots are the direct cause for the arising of karma (A.1.264), with a distinctly ethical function, infatuating the mind (*cetaso sārāgo*) with "things" (*dhamme*) that are grounded on evil desire and excitement (*chandarāgaṭṭhānīye*). But of all the groups, the cankers are primus inter pares because they are the most embedded and the last group of harmful dispositions to be overcome in the process of enlightenment (A.4.448). Frequently spoken of as the root of ignorance, they are the major obstacle to the acknowledgement of the four Truths. And although the dormant tendencies, unwholesome roots, and cankers are emphasized for varying and different reasons in psychological, ethical, and "theological" contexts, they all refer to unconscious dispositional forces that contribute to the arising of craving.

In explicating the background of craving a psychological picture with a two-fold emphasis has emerged. On the one hand, just as the Buddha rejects substance theories of the body, so does he reject a substance account of mind. Mind is discussed in psychological and dispositional terms only. On the other hand, as has been argued throughout this chapter, the principal psychological dimension which conditions the dispositional destiny of mind is seen to be craving and its related roots. Regarded as a purely psychological phenomenon in the Western way, craving might be discussed by the psychologist as a question only of motivation. But for the Buddhist craving as a conative force has a strategic religious significance as well.

The next chapter shows further that salvation in Theravāda Buddhism depends upon the achievement of right intention, and the harnessing of craving plays a major role in this. Far from curbing or eroding the will, Buddhism asks that all volition, including craving (*taṇhā*), be purified in order to arrive at a will of higher quality. This makes possible the realization of freedom from the self-centered forms of craving and the roots that feed it. By keeping this crucial issue in mind craving takes on the added dimension of being more than a topic of a psychological interest, and its religious place in Buddhist life and thought stands in a new light.

Chapter 3

CRAVING AND EMANCIPATION

In the last chapter an analysis of the infrastructure of craving showed how, to use the graphic imagery of M.1.271, the mind becomes entangled in the "great net of thirst" (*mahātaṇhājāla*). It demonstrated how craving arises and what effects it has on the individual in *saṃsāra*. The present task is to investigate the way of release from this net, the way to emancipation.

There are here two different but nonetheless related problems. First, to use the language of the *Itivuttaka* (114), to see how Buddhism seeks to divert "the current of craving" from harmful thirsts to more ethical and intellectual objectives. Here it can be demonstrated that far from being a pessimistic soteriology, Buddhism in fact urges the development of the senses and the application of energy and wholesome or skillful (*kusala*) intention to pursue a freedom from craving and the coarser forms of volition. Second, the matter of the relationship between purified volition and the practice of meditation must be reviewed since these two factors share an interesting association.

The central argument is that both will and mind are religiously important, and that mindfulness and meditation must first be seen as being dependent upon a "theology of will" or intention, which forms the most general basis of emancipation in Buddhism. This is not a universally accepted position in Buddhist studies. Many interpreters underestimate the complex efficacy of conation or willing in Buddhism, and this sort of emphasis has often led to a negative assessment. Before anything else is said on this matter it is necessary to define what is meant by will as it is laid down in the Sutta Piṭaka.

1. The Buddhist Concept of Will

In the West, with its traditional psychological categories of cognition, conation, and affection, the will has frequently been pigeon-holed as a problem of conation only. Many theorists[1] have argued that this classical structure is artificial, and that in fact cognition (perceiving, judging, reasoning), conation (exertion, struggle, volition), and affection (mood, emotion, temperament), if they exist at all as separate categories,[2] overlap in so many places as to make distinctions between them blurred. I am in essential agreement with this criticism, and, in my investigation of a concept of will in the Sutta Piṭaka, I have found that the most persuasive and useful definition is one that straddles the traditional conative, affective, and cognitive roles, that embraces such terms as *viriya* (energy, striving), *chanda* (desire, intention), and *dvārāni suguttāni* (guarding the doors of the senses).

This definition may be justified by arguing that, if will is categorized as simply energy or striving, much of its moral and essentially ethical nature is lost; and likewise, if it is categorized only in ethical terms, it loses that sense of positive drive so apparent in much of the Buddhist *magga* or spiritual path. Western students of Buddhism have frequently failed to recognize, with sometimes disastrous interpretive results, that the concept of will has these dimensions. The mischief begins with Arthur Schopenhauer (1788-1860), whose own celebrated doctrine of the will as an "unquenchable thirst"[3] approximates his notion of the Buddhist concept of craving. The fact that Schopenhauer was recognized to be at least partially indebted to the Buddhist *dhamma*, and the fact that he was responsible for introducing some idea of what the nature of Buddhist psychology was to a Europe still very much in the dark about the mysteries of Eastern thought, helped to identify the Buddhist concept of the will with his own pessimistic account.

The impression that willing in Buddhism is always associated with thirst or desire, and that desire in turn is always deleterious, was reinforced by the early translations of the Pāli texts into European languages. C. A. F. Rhys Davids points this out in one of her best and most creative essays, "On the Will in Buddhism."[4] In a comparison of various English translations with the originals she observes that "the one English word 'desire' is made to do duty for no less than seventeen Pāli words, for example, *taṇhā* (craving), *ākāsam* (space, "puffed-up state"), *visattikaṃ* (dart of lust), *chātatā* (hunger), *sita* (clinging)...not one of which means desire taken in its ordinary general sense, but rather in that of perverted, morbid, excessive desire."[5] She found also that much was the same case with the French and German translations of Burnouf, Foucaud, Oldenberg, Müller, Fausböll, and Neumann. For these translators, desire in the context of the Sutta Piṭaka was always bad, though in the West it had not lost its equivocal moral connotation. C. A. F. Rhys Davids further emphasizes that the languages which developed within the legacy of Western philosophy "do not afford equivalents for Oriental standpoints" and that this is particularly serious when one approaches the Buddhist attitude "in relation to the volitional side of the human mind."[6] She insists that even those familiar with the Indian languages do not exercise enough care in distinguishing among psychological words which have closely parallel but not synonymous meanings. She reminds us that, when the Pāli Canon wishes to convey ethical values in terms of willing, either distinct and special words are used, or the expression of willing is explicitly qualified as referring to an object of perverted desire or to "a morbid state of will." Thus, want or wish (*ākankhā*) becomes craving (*taṇhā*), desire (*chanda*) becomes lust (*chandarāga*), love (*kāma*) becomes lust (*kāmarāga*) or sensual delight (*nandirāga*).

By pointing out how complicated an issue will is in the Sutta Piṭaka, and how inconsistent most Western interpreters of the Buddhist texts are when it comes to translating Pāli words related to the general idea of willing (*cetanā*, *viriya*, *taṇhā*, etc.), C. A. F. Rhys Davids has made an important cautionary statement. The major contribution of her essay, however, lies in her suggestion that will as such, and desire as such, are not to be repressed, but that their cultivation is "absolutely indispensable to any advance towards the attainment of Buddhist ideals."[7] Having said this, she lashes out against Schopenhauer and those whom she suspects of casting Buddhism, even unwittingly, in the distasteful and misleading mould of pessimism.[8] By arguing that neither will nor the "preciousness of life" can be said to be repressed in Buddhism, C. A. F. Rhys Davids shows that, as a soteriology, Buddhism seeks "to foster and strengthen aspiration and resolve in the effort to persevere towards complete attainment of what it held to be the noblest kind of life."

Students of Buddhism today would be well-advised to consider what Mrs. Rhys Davids proposes in this important but neglected article. What she has said has been ignored or forgotten. That same negative attitude towards will in Buddhism that C. A. F. Rhys Davids encountered in 1897 persists in more recent studies. For example, Arnold Toynbee asserts that "inward peace" in Buddhism looks "unattainable" since desires cannot be given up without cultivating the desire to give them up,[9] and further that Buddhism enjoined "the suppression of desires that are ordinarily regarded as being altruistic, such as love and pity." Likewise Dhammasuddhi observes, "so long as there is will, freedom cannot exist. Will, itself is conditioned by selfish desire, attachment, ignorance of truth and so on.... Freedom...means freedom from the will.[10] Or again, when D. K. Swearer writes, "where the biblical tradition focuses on man's will in its interpretation of the human situation, Buddhism focuses on man's mind,"[11] he appears to emphasize only one aspect of the soteriological problem, and consequently of its solution.

2. The Affirmative Character of Buddhist Conative Psychology

This outlook is firmly expressed in the texts. The whole perspective of the Buddhist path is based to a considerable degree on positive willing. In the Eightfold Path (*aṭṭhangiko maggo*) the first factor in the so-called meditation or *samādhi* section[12] is right effort (*sammā-vāyāma*) which indicates that the mental energy of proper intention and desire undergird meditation: "And what, your reverences, is right effort? As to this...a monk generates desire, endeavours, stirs up energy, exerts his mind (*cittaṃ*), and strives for the non-arising of evil unskilled states," M.3.251.[13]

Other factors of the Eightfold Path also point to actions that demand resolve and positive intention (i.e., right speech, action, and livelihood). Nor is the Eightfold Path the only formulation of the importance of will in the search for freedom. For example, in another list known as the thirty-seven qualities belonging to awakening (*bodhipakkhiyā dhammā*) set forth by the Buddha at Vesali just before he died (D.2.119f.), the emphasis is evenly divided between the will to acquire enlightenment and the method of meditation.

In another way the Sutta Piṭaka emphasizes the significance of positive conation. This is seen in the clear distinction it makes between unwholesome (*akusala*) and wholesome (*kusala*) desire and volition. This is notably the case with the many synonyms for craving (*taṇhā*). The last chapter referred to the "adhesive strip" of *taṇhā*, which describes a number of synonymous volitional factors. These, like *taṇhā*, bind consciousness (*viññāṇa*), mind (*mano*), and "personality" (*citta*) to ignorance and *saṃsāra*. So in M.3.32 we find *chanda* (lust, striving), *rāga* (passion), *upādāna* (grasping) and *anusaya* (inclination), all used synonymously with *taṇhā*. There are as well other lists, such as D.3.238, where *pipāsā* (thirst) and *pariḷāha* (fever of passion) are used synonymously with craving, and in M.1.270 *nandī* (feeling of delight), like craving, is said to come just before grasping in the Series of Dependencies.

Some of these synonyms, notably *rāga* and *pariḷāha*, are never used in a positive conative sense. There are, though, instances where both *taṇhā* and the other synonyms are used positively to express the reformation and cultivation of will and desire.

3. Changing the Current of Desire: *Taṇhā* as "Wholesome" (*kusala*) Craving

Craving (*taṇhā*) itself is not often used in this kind of positive context, but there are one or two interesting uses of the word which show that it was not always employed to indicate an unwholesome situation. An important example is found in D.3.216 in which the three kinds of craving normally discussed in the Sutta Piṭaka (craving for pleasure, for life, and for death, S.5.421) are further added to:

> Three other directions of craving (*aparā pi tisso taṇhā*) are craving for sensuality, for life in this material world, and for life in the higher worlds (*arūpa taṇhā*). Again, three other directions of craving are craving for life in this world, for life in the higher worlds, and craving for cessation (*nirodha taṇhā*).

Controversy surrounds the meaning of *nirodha taṇhā*. T. W. Rhys Davids maintains that it should be taken in the sense of "craving for life to end, the Uccheda or Annihilationist view."[14] Johansson concludes that it refers to craving for the cessation of everything that is negative. This provokes him to remark that "even *taṇhā* can be a desirable motive."[15] Others maintain that it refers to a more noble, albeit paradoxical, cravving for nirvāṇa. This view is supported by a later valuable text (*Netti-pakaraṇa* 87) which makes this observation:

> Here, craving is of two kinds (*taṇhā duvidhā*), skillful and unskillful (profitable or unprofitable—*kusalā pi akusalā pi*). While the unprofitable kind goes with *saṃsāra*, the profitable kind leads to the giving up of craving. Take for example the case of the grief that has as its cause the renunciation (*nekkhammaṃ*) of craving. It is described thus: "When shall I enter upon and abide in that base, which peaceful base the Noble Ones enter upon and abide in?" And longing arises in him, and grief with the longing as its condition: such craving is profitable; for there is freedom of mind (*citta*) due to the fading of lust (*rāgavirāgā cetovimutti*). Such craving is profitable in having that for its object.

This passage lends definite support to the argument that craving for nirvāṇa was taken to be at least partially beneficial from a soteriological point of view. Another text of unusual interest is A.2.144, sometimes referred to as the Nun's Sutta. Here Ananda instructs a nun (*bhikkhunī*) about the ultimate goal of release from craving in this interesting way:

> Sister, as to the saying "this body has come into being through craving, is dependent on craving; craving must be abandoned"—it was said in this connection. Herein, sister, a monk hears it said: "They say that such and such a monk, by destroying the cankers, and in this present life thoroughly comprehending it, realizes the mind's (*ceto*) release, the release by wisdom, that it is free from the cankers, and having attained it he abides therein." To him it occurs: "surely I too, by destroying the cankers...having attained it shall abide therein." Then sometime later, though dependent on craving, he abandons craving (*so aparena samayena taṇhaṃ nissāya taṇhaṃ pajahati*).

Although this passage is certain that in the long run craving is to be abandoned, it can be argued that the word "*nissāya*" (*ni* + *śri*—that on which one depends) instructs us that release from craving initially relies upon craving for its release.[16] Jayatilleke goes further and maintains that here we should distinguish between "self-centred desires" and a so-called "master desire" for nirvāṇa which "is not on the same footing as the first order desires." The master desire, he adds, eliminates the self-centred desires, until both orders of craving are distinguished in the attainment of complete awareness.[17]

In contemporary Theravāda Buddhism one seldom finds craving spoken of as a positive force. It is almost always associated with evil (*pāpa*), especially by monks. Clearly this is a case of custom investing a certain term (*taṇhā*) with a specific application acquired over centuries. But in the early texts, as has been shown, there are occasions when craving is used with a more positive sense. Curiously, amongst a number of lay devotees I have found a greater openness to this usage.[18] What does need to be emphasized is that the texts nowhere assert that craving is an end in itself in the realization of nirvāṇa. The passages just examined (D.3.216, Nett. 87, A.2.114) show that positive (*kusala*, *nissāya*) craving can at best be seen as a stepping-stone to getting rid of craving altogether.

The same can be said of grasping (*upādāna*), a close synonym of *taṇhā*, which is sometimes referred to as the positive though somewhat misdirected zeal that urges one to progress in meditation:

> Ananda, a monk who has grasping does not attain to nirvāṇa. "But where, revered sir, does a monk grasp who is grasping?" The plane of neither-perception nor non-perception Ananda. "Indeed, sir, the monk who is grasping grasps after the best of graspings." That monk who is grasping grasps after the best of graspings, Ananda. For this is the best of graspings (*upādānaseṭṭham*) Ananda, that is to say the plane of neither-perception nor non-perception. M.2.265

The best of graspings (*upādānaseṭṭha*) occurs in the advanced state of meditation called the eighth *jhāna* (*nevasaññānāsaññayātana*). But only after this, in the "crowning experience" wherein consciousness and sensation are stilled (*saññāvedayitanirodha*), are the cankers (*āsavā*) finally eradicated (i.e., D.2.97). Craving and grasping after nirvāṇa are at best a feature of the early stages of meditation. They are left aside only in the most advanced levels of meditation. This sort of craving for awareness is good in the sense that it is not preverted or morbid, but it is of course part of man's inadequately developed insight into the goal of awareness.

4. The Dynamics of Willing (*Chanda*)

So far we have reviewed texts which show how craving (*taṇhā*) or unwholesome thirst can be changed into a thirst to overcome that unwholesomeness. Although this purified kind of craving is not part of the experience of nirvāṇa, the important point at issue is that craving may nonetheless be used affirmatively in the pursuit of salvation. The "current" of craving can be diverted; desire as such is not to be repressed but cultivated and developed and used for a positive end. This position is supported by the way the Sutta Piṭaka uses the noun *chanda*. *Chanda* derives from the Sanskrit verb "to jump," meaning intention, ambition, desire. It is one of the most versatile conative words in Pāli. Although *chanda* is frequently used as a synonym for unwholesome craving (for instance in S.5.272), it is also often used to indicate part of the path leading to nirvāṇa (M.2.173). This ambiguity is everywhere apparent in the texts,[19] for example S.5.272, where *chanda* is first censured as gross craving, and then encouraged as that kind of desire that leads to *arahant*-ship (perfected state of awareness):

> So seated the brahmin Unnabha said this to the venerable Ananda: "What is it, master Ananda, for which the holy life is lived under Gotama the recluse?" "For the sake of abandoning desire (*chandapahānatthaṃ*) brahmin, the holy life is lived under the

> Blessed One." "But is there any way, is there any practice, master Ananda, for abandoning this desire?" "There is a way, brahmin, there is a practice for abandoning this desire.... Herein, brahmin, a monk cultivates the four bases of psychic power (*iddhipādam*), of which the features are desire (*chanda*), together with the factors of meditation (*samādhi*) and struggle (*padhāna*); also that of energy (*viriya*) and "thought" (*citta*) in meditation, and that of investigation, together with the factors of meditation and struggle. This, brahmin, is the way, this is the practice for the abandoning of this sensual desire." "If that be so, master Ananda, it were a task without end (*santakaṃ*), not one with an end. That he should get rid of one desire by means of another desire seems an impossible thing." "Then, brahmin, I will question you in this matter. Answer as you think right." "Now, brahmin, what do you think? Previously, was there not a desire in you urging you thus: "I will go to the park?" When you get to the park, was not that appropriate desire calmed?" "Yes, master"...[then follow several other examples of desire leading to a fruitful result and thus being satiated]. "Very well then, brahmin. That monk who is aware, one in whom the cankers are destroyed, who has lived the life, done the task, lifted the burden, who is a winner of his own welfare, who has outworn the fetters of rebirth, one who is released by perfect insight—that desire which he had previously to attain awareness (literally, *arahattapattiyā*), now that emancipation is won, that appropriate (*tajjo*) desire is calmed (*paṭippassaddho*)."

The most striking point here is that coarse desire has been canalized to another sort of desire which in the end is not to be characterized in terms of liquidation or expurgation but as that which can be allayed, quieted (*paṭippassaddha*). The emotional and volitional features of *chanda* are not paralyzed; they are developed and refined, incorporated into the path of salvation.

The significance given to *chanda* in this path varies from text to text. In the foregoing passage and elsewhere *chanda* is closely involved with meditation itself, as in S.5.268.[20] In other places (M.1.480, 2.173) *chanda* is judged to be part of a process which leads to enlightenment. Stress is placed far more on striving and energy than on meditation:

> When trust is born (*saddhājāto*), he, having approached and sitting with the teacher, thus sitting turns his ear, and after listening to the law (*dhammaṃ*), and having heard it he holds it in mind; he then examines the meaning of the law which he has held in mind and having examined its meaning and understanding it, he is able to approve (*khamanti*) of it. The desire (*chando*) is born along with patience in understanding the law. Desire being born, (such a man) makes an effort (*ussahati*); having made an effort, he considers (*tūleti*); having considered he strives (*padahati*); having striven, indeed with his own body, he experiences the highest truth and sees it, having pierced it (*ativijjha*) with his wisdom (*paññāya*). M.2.173

There is nothing negative about the function and purpose of desire in this account of the process of conversion. The failure of many early critics to recognize the crucial role *chanda* plays in Buddhist perfection provoked C. A. F. Rhys Davids to remark:

> Now we cannot afford to impoverish our ethical (and aesthetical) concepts by squandering this term (*chanda*) outright on (gross) *taṇhā*, and thereby, so to speak, make the devil a present of all desire—even of that *dhamma chanda*... that drove the Buddha from home to Bo-tree. Much harm hereby has been wrought by translators, whose cheapening of the word "desire" has justified the superficial criticism which perennially speaks of Buddhist ethics as the "negation" or "extinction" of all desire.[21]

The "theology of intention" that we have been developing concurs with the judgment of Mrs. Rhys Davids. This argument also finds support in contemporary Buddhist scholarship. Thus Malalasekera observes: "It is not freedom from desire as such, but freedom from enslavement to blind and shifting desires."[22] In a similar vein Jayatilleke remarks that it is a freedom "which consists in changing the basis of our motivation from greed, hatred and ignorance to selfless service, compassion and understanding."[23] A careful reading of the Sutta Piṭaka supports these opinions and declares that the Buddha did not hold up as an example of emancipation an individual totally disengaged from all volitional response and certain human needs. Nor was the way to enlightenment said to be a way of repression. Unwholesome desires are to be understood and then eradicated, but the energy of desire is not to be expurgated. It is, rather, to be redirected towards higher, more positive ethical and intellectual intentions, thus contributing to the attainment of enlightenment.

5. Development of the Senses (*Indriyāni*)

The Sutta Piṭaka urges that, as volition is purged of its moral impurities and redirected to higher purposes, the senses should not be led to atrophy but brought under control and developed. The teaching also urges the cultivation of a new attitude towards the senses, a recognition of how they may contribute to the nature of volitional response. When the operation of the senses has been understood, one attempts to master the stimulation of the senses and regulate the quality of volition.

Initially the individual must understand how the senses provoke unwholesome craving. The Sutta Piṭaka is explicit about the close relation between the senses and craving. There is an example of this in A.1.1., where lust (*kāmataṇhā*), built upon excitation of all the senses, is said to affect the whole "personality" (*citta*):

> The Blessed One said: monks, I know not of any other single body by which the *citta* of a man is attracted as it is by that of a woman. I know not of any other single sound by which the *citta* is so attracted as it is by the voice of a woman. I know of no

> other single smell...flavour... touch by which the *citta* is attracted as it is by the smell, flavour, and touch of a woman.

Many other passages in the Sutta Piṭaka point up the grip that the senses can have over the mind (D.1.26, S.4.15, M.1.15, 85, 2.253). Once the senses have been analyzed and their dangers marked out (Dhm. 362f.) the seeker has a responsibility to recognize the need to struggle against the forceful but ill-directed current of craving which has been excited by the senses. The bond that exists between the senses and craving, and the necessity of reducing their controlling power over the individual, is clearly set out in the celebrated Parable of the Man in the River (Itv. 114):

> Suppose a man is carried along in a river by a current which looks delightful and charming. Then a sharp-sighted man standing on the bank seeing him calls out: "Good man, though you are carried along in the river by a current which looks delightful and charming, yet further down here is a pool with waves and whirlpools, with monsters and demons. When you get there you will come to your death or painfulness." Then, that man, hearing the other's call, struggles against the stream with hands and feet. This figure, I use to explain my meaning. And in this case the meaning is: "a river current" is a name for craving; "looking delightful and charming" is a name of one's own sphere of perception; "the pool lower down" is a name for the five fetters (*saṃyojanānaṃ*) belonging to this lower world. "With waves" is a name for the five pleasures of sense. "With monsters and demons" is a name for women (*mātugāmassetaṃ*). Monks, "against the stream" is a name for freedom from craving. "Struggle (*viriyārambhassetaṃ*) with hands and feet" is a name for the exercise of energy. And "the sharp-sighted man standing on the bank" is a name for the Tathāgata, the *arahant*, the perfectly Enlightened One.

Here the emphasis centers on the struggle of energy (*viriya*)[24] needed to overcome craving and its reliance upon the senses. This terminology seems to indicate the need for a right volitional attitude in coming to grips with the senses. It is important to point out that in this text there is no suggestion that the aim of the struggle is to deaden the senses. The very analogy of a struggle has to do with cultivation and development rather than neutralization. Above all the individual learns to separate cognition from thirst. He learns also to liberate the senses from servitude to craving. He does not let his senses fall away but perceives that when the senses stimulate egocentric craving they present a counterfeit world which ignores the characteristics of the world's impermanence. Thus the way of salvation is also the way of right cognition. Right cognition sees not only transiency and painfulness but that the senses contribute to all notions of self-interest, and indeed recognizes that this is a spiritual hazard. The one who is aware of this has a constant responsibility to keep watch on his senses. The reward is ultimate freedom from craving:

> Eye, ear, nose, tongue and body and also the mind, if a monk keeps these gates guarded well (*dvārāni suguttāni*), in eating with restraint and control, in meeting with ease the sense faculties, with ease of body and with ease of mind (*cetosukhaṃ*). With a body that does not burn (i.e., with thirst), with a mind that does not burn, he lives at ease by day and night. Itv. 24

This passage warrants a detailed exegesis of the phrase *dvārāni suguttāni* (guarding the "doors," viz. the senses) in order to bring out its significance. Here the gates (*dvāra*) refer to the sense organs, what has been appropriately described as the "in-and-outlets of the mind."[25] *Sugguttāni* as well means "well-guarded," "watchful," "constrained." Certainly this passage should not be interpreted to mean that life must be devoid of all sense pleasure. There are texts which plainly point out that even for monks not all sense pleasures are to be considered dangerous. M.3.230, for example, indicates:

> Whatever is happiness in association with sense pleasures and intentness on a joy that is low, of the villager (*gammaṃ*), of the average man, undistinguished (*anariyaṃ*), not connected with the goal, this is something which has misery, painfulness, trouble, and anguish, and it is a wrong course. But whatever is happiness in association with sense pleasures but with no intent on a joy that is low, of the villager and average man not connected with the goal, this is something without misery, painfulness, trouble or anguish; it is the right path to walk on (*sammāpaṭipadā*).

The emancipated one (*arahant*) has a new attitude towards the use of the senses and the kinds of satisfaction they give. Such a person never deliberately destroys or represses sense functions but refines them and uses them as instruments to see behind the world of ignorance. There are doubtless some critics who do not accept such an interpretation. They might appeal to certain texts in the Sutta Piṭaka, such as Dhm. 360, which seem to indicate a possible crushing of the senses rather than developing them.

It would be a misinterpretation of one of the major foci of Buddhism to read into any text a concept of "cutting off" of the senses. As will later become clear, even in enlightenment there is still activity of the senses; there are still experiences of physical pain and pleasure. But at this stage, freed from egocentric craving, sensory stimulation of any kind has no real effect on spiritual equilibrium. One is neither troubled nor excited by the senses because complete control of their activity and their volitional resonance has been gained.

In other words, the *arahant* engages the senses; he continues to receive their record but remains detached from them. At this level the senses are as if by "second nature" constrained from unwholesome willing, and the *arahant* enters into nirvāṇa:

> Here, monks, a monk is meritorious (*arahaṃ*), one who has destroyed the cankers, who has lived the life, done what was to be done, laid down the burden, won the goal, worn out

> the fetter of becoming, one released by perfect knowledge. In him the five sense faculties still remain, through which, as they have not yet departed, he experiences sensations both pleasant and unpleasant, experiences pleasure and painfulness. In him the end of lust, hatred, and delusion, monks, is called the condition of nirvāṇa with the basis (i.e., the senses—*saupādisesā*) still remaining. Itv. 38

To this point it has been made clear that Buddhism teaches the overcoming of pathogenic responses to evil intentions by means of wholesome volition and a proper development of the senses. We have seen how the *arahant* still acts from positive motivation such as love and compassion, how he is still active (*ātāpin*), but, because he is without craving, he is emotionally "cool" (*sītabhūta* Sn. 642), and accordingly his cognitive processes also become more objective and realistic (A.3.378). It has been argued that one of the principal aims in Buddhism is the redirection, and not the suffocation, of the energy of volition and of the operation of the sense faculties.

There is yet another side to this "theology of intention," namely, its relation to meditation. To this we now turn.

6. Craving and Meditation

That Buddhism is a religion securely based on a great tradition of meditation is unquestionable. Within this discipline the heart of the Buddha's saving message is revealed. The significance of meditation as part of the path to salvation in Buddhism cannot be overestimated.

As the complexities of Buddhist meditation are confronted, it must be with the understanding that meditation begins fruitfully and meaningfully only when there is right intention towards emancipation. The development of proper volition and the control of the senses is critical to the success of meditation. In this section, however, we want to demonstrate that, although meditation partly depends on the will to "tame the monkey of the mind" (S.2.94) and thereby change the direction of conduct, the final aim is to achieve the disposition which proceeds from wisdom (*paññā*).

Two points will be developed. First we want to see how the Sutta Piṭaka gradually shifts the salvational emphasis from the conative to the noetic. Here the aim is to examine the discipline of the moral life and the processes of meditation as set forth in the texts. Second, there is more to know about the nature of wisdom (*paññā*) in the soteriological process. In what way does wisdom or "insight" draw upon an understanding of the role of conation, and how is it that in *paññā*, craving and all forms of volition are eventually brought to an end? The discussion must go beyond the criteria associated with the formative stages of spiritual life (conduct and meditation), and will be concerned with the existential purpose and spiritual aim of the path as it is expressed in the "limbs" of wisdom (right understanding and thought, *sammādiṭṭhi*, *sammāsankappa*). For here the path describes the unique experience of the *arahant*. Although it is perhaps harder to analyze than the ethical and meditational background, the discussion of wisdom finally gets to the heart of the Buddhist understanding of craving and its relation to salvation.

To begin, reference can be made to those texts such as D.1.62f, and M.1.200, 346, which outline a method leading to awareness. This consists of the three stages of morality, meditation, and insight in the Eightfold Path. As we have already intimated, whether this numerical system was schematically contrived or not, its practical aim is to remove in an orderly way impediments to the development of meditation and concentration. It is not surprising that the initial emphasis of the Eightfold Path should be upon morality or virtue (*sīla*). It is taken to be essential for success in meditation and for pursuit of the final fruit of wisdom —something casual or "experimental" meditators may not take seriously enough ("morality is washed around with wisdom and wisdom with morality"—*sīla-paridhotā...paññā, paññā-paridhotaṃ sīlaṃ*," D.1.124).

The Sutta Piṭaka is explicit about what makes up virtue (*sīla*). Usually it is associated with the five precepts (*pañca sīla*) of the layman, and the ten (*dasa*) precepts reserved for monks or, as Saddhatissa puts it, "for the more pious of the laity who could remain unattached to their families."[26] Apart from the morality of the Eightfold Path, comprehensive lists are provided guarding against killing (*pāṇātipāta veramaṇī*), stealing (*adinnādāna*), sexual misconduct (*kāmesu micchācāra*), lying (*musāvāda*), intemperance (*surāmeraya*). These are the "five precepts." Other precepts augment this. They also proscribe speech that is slanderous (*pisuṇāvācā*), impolite (*pharusāvācā*), or frivolous (*samphappalāpa*); covetousness (*abhijjhā*); malevolence (*byāpāda*); and heretical views (*micchādiṭṭhi*).[27] In M.1.345 these virtues are set in the context of a positive exposition of the good life for the one who can adhere to them. Such a person is usually a monk or a novice (*sāmaṇera*) willing to abstain from violence and impropriety of any kind, from harming even seed and vegetable growth. He speaks only with discrimination (*sāpadesa*) and taste, avoiding egocentric or frivolous talk. Understandably, his wants must be few; but with these virtues he is as free as a "bird on the wing" (*pakkhī sakuṇo*) and, taking these things with him wherever he goes (D.1.71), having this "noble body of virtuousness" (*ariyena sīlakkhandhena*), he lives blameless, with mind cleansed of covetousness (*abhijjhāya cittaṃ parisodheti*). Certainly virtue as described here refers to a wholesome conative attitude in the ordering of life. It supposes that one does not start with a good conduct automatically, but one must work at it with discipline and energy. By itself, however, virtue cannot produce wisdom. It can at best provide merit (*puñña*), even though it becomes part of a causal chain and in this way contributes to the process which culminates in wisdom.

For the Buddha, of much greater significance than the actual performance of virtue was the intention underlying virtuous conduct. Thus in the continuation of M.1.345 (and in other texts as well, for instance, M.1.145f and 3.129f) we are told that the virtuous life leads to restraint of the senses (*indriyasaṃvara*), which in turn causally conditions the development of mindfulness (*satisampajañña*), and thence the arising of wisdom.

Although the Buddha (and all contemporary Buddhists I have worked with) urge self-control and the exercise of will power in the pursuit of a wholesome ethical life, it should be emphasized that this is not for any ascetic or puritanical motive. Rather, it is always informed by the ultimate ambition of training the mind through meditation. Here the senses are controlled, resentment and other hindrances of will removed, unconscious roots of malevolent conduct understood and thus destroyed, and craving of any kind dissolved. This is efficacious only as success is attained in the contemplation of reality, in cutting through ignorance and experiencing for oneself the great truths of impermanency. Without the final accomplishment of wisdom or insight (*paññā*), meditation, even at its highest level, cannot yield enlightenment—the cankers cannot be completely eradicated, and the craving disposition will sooner or later resurface.

7. Techniques of Meditation

Turning to the mechanics of meditation, one finds in both Theravāda tradition and practice an interesting variety of methods. Others have written extensively on this theme, either from a classical point of view[28] or from the perspective of contemporary schools of meditation in South and Southeast Asia.[29] A few recent studies have attempted to do both with considerable perception, notably those by Nyanaponika, D. K. Swearer, and Winston King. This is not the place to give a comprehensive review of such a complex subject, but some observations are necessary in order to build a framework in which the ultimate evaluation of craving can be better understood.

Most informed Buddhists accept the existence of a certain tension in the meditational structure of their religion because of the bifurcation of practice indicated in the seventh and eighth factors of the Eightfold Path, namely *sati* (mindfulness) and *samādhi* (concentration). These terms, however, are not always used. In reading the texts and in discussing meditation with contemporary practitioners, one finds synonyms as well, something that at first can lead to confusion. This is more evident with the appearance of the term *vipassanā* (insight) as the goal of mindfulness (*sati*), and of the term *jhāna* (absorption or trace) to describe the process of meditation (*samādhi*, as in A.2.157). Frequently one will hear or read of the "*vipassanā-jhāna*" dichotomy in Buddhist meditational practice. This merely refers to the more traditional classification of mindfulness and meditation (*sati-samādhi*).

Another way in which this difference is expressed is found in references such as A.1.437f, which denotes freedom through the mind (*cetovimutti*), on the one hand, and freedom through intuitive wisdom (*paññāvimutti*) on the other. Thus one who "goes after calm," as the text remarks, is called "freed in mind" (as in *samādhi*), and one who successfully pursues wisdom is called "freed through wisdom" (as in *sati*). The Buddha himself pointed out that both ways are valid and meaningful, and one might choose a particular method according to one's needs or faculties (*indriyavemattatā*). Furthermore, the texts and the modern tradition allow for the practice of both ways together (D.2.71—*ubhatobhāgavimutto*). And, on the odd occasion, there is even reference to freedom being gained without any formal meditational practice. In M.3.20 listeners to the *dhamma* are said to have been emancipated (*vimuccimsūti*) on the spot. This is consistent with the Buddhist doctrine of faith (*saddhā*) in the *dhamma*, a faith which is, as Robinson puts it, "the seed which grows into confirmatory realization...a willingness to take statements provisionally on trust, confidence in the integrity of a witness, and determination to practise according to instructions."[30]

The central point here is that, despite variations of procedure or method, Buddhist meditation has a definite structure. In a recent important contribution to this subject, Winston King puts forward the argument that these procedures reflect the historical links Buddhist meditational practices have with the Yogic-Brahmanic tradition. He goes on to demonstrate that the way of *samādhi* (concentration leading to calmness) is distinctly Yogic, but the way of *vipassanā* (or *sati*—mindfulness leading to insight) is more specifically Buddhist. He sees this tension in such seemingly contradictory passages as M.1.121 and 1.242, in which devotees are instructed on the one hand to work hard at their meditation (drawing on the Hindu ascetic model) and, on the other hand, simply to be mindful. King rightly labels this as "Gotama's acceptance—rejection of contemporary spiritual techniques."[31] This discussion leads him to conclude that the way of *samādhi* (or at least part of it) is something inherited from the Indian tradition from which the Buddha and his followers came, and that instead of rejecting this method of meditation the Buddha incorporated it into his own evolving way of *vipassanā* or insight through mindfulness.

These remarks on technique provide a vital basis from which any discussion of meditation should proceed. If any early conclusions can be drawn from them, it is that both ways are available and in fact work together to provide the insight and equilibrium necessary for ultimate freedom from craving. In the long run it is questionable whether nirvāṇa can be obtained only through meditation (*samādhi*) or the calming stages of its so-called "absorptions" (*jhāna*). Despite the fact that some texts (M.1.437) seem to indicate that *samādhi* by itself can lead to freedom (*vimutti*), traditionally and in modern Buddhist theory most teachers argue that *sati* (mindfulness) alone can lead to insight and nirvāṇa.

What are some of the major differences between these two meditational ways? And where does craving fit into this? It has been noted that mindfulness can lead to insight and thence to nirvāṇa by itself, without the help of the calming benefits of meditation. This gives mindfulness a unique priority in meditational methods. This is apparent when one reads the two great chapters in the Sutta Piṭaka that refer to mindfulness, notably M.1.55f and D.2.290f (the Satipaṭṭhāna Suttas). Here one is instructed to be mindful of that which appears to constitute the whole person, in particular the body and its feelings, perceptions, and thoughts. By deep reflection on these properties the individual comes first to recognize transiency for what it is:

> As to the body (*kāye*), he continues to consider (*anupassī*) it, either externally or internally, or both. He keeps on considering how the body is something that comes to be, or again how the body is something that passes away; or again he keeps on considering that coming to be with that passing away; or again, conscious that "there is the body," mindfulness here becomes established, deep enough for the purposes of knowledge (*ñāna-mattāya*) and of mindfulness and he lives independent, grasping after nothing whatever in the world. D.2.292

One achieves this state of mindfulness, for example, by contemplating on the breathing function (*ānāpānasati*) of the body. Unlike some breathing exercises of Hindu *hatha* yoga, there is in this distinctly Buddhist procedure no interference with the breathing process. Apart from the probable psychological benefit of calming the agitated mind, meditation on breathing offers an obvious insight into momentariness (*anicca*), as Nyanaponika observes when he writes:

> Just as, in ancient mystical thought, breath was identified with the life force itself, so does Buddhist tradition regard breathing as representative of the bodily functions (*kāya-sankharā*). In the obvious evanescence of breath we perceive the impermanence of the body; in heavy, short, or strained breath, or in the ailments of the respiratory organs, we become aware of the suffering associated with the body.[32]

The same purpose of perceiving transiency lies behind mindfulness of the organic parts of the body, of its composition from the four primary elements, and even of the contemplation of corpses in various stages of decay (D.2.294). As with mindfulness of the body, so too are the exercises of contemplating feelings (*vedanānupassanā*), states of mind (*cittānupassanā*), and mental contexts (*dhammānupassanā*) aimed at intuitively perceiving and accepting the impermanent nature of the self. These exercises also serve to disengage consciousness from craving after worthless satisfaction for a body which has no permanent value. Likewise they penetrate the unconscious roots of behaviour and attitude,[33] delving, as M.3.125 suggests, into the causes for the arising of greed (*abhijjhā*), hatred (*byāpāda*), and malevolence (*vihiṃsā*). Similarly, in another text (S.4.112), mindfulness is described as perceiving "the evil and unskilled processes" (*pāpakā akusalā dhammā*) that lie behind want and discontent.

Aside from the insight which mindfulness provides about transiency, there is a second conclusion: mindfulness is the instrument by which conscious and unconscious craving are to be understood and dissolved. Correct application of mindfulness can lead to a state of volitional purification and intuitive awareness in which craving and emotion of any kind are eliminated and their causal potency neutralized. Such a state, if profound enough, can indeed bring about the destruction of the cankers (S.2.54) and so admit the seeker to nirvāṇa.

The mindfulness (*sati*) procedure of meditation is unique to Buddhism and is completely consistent with the Buddhist world-view, based as it is on insight into momentariness and appearance. But although *sati* can lead by itself to nirvāṇa, it is not uncommon to find it practised along with the more Yogic method of *samādhi* (meditation or concentration). A.2.157 points out that one meditational procedure does not necessarily have to come before the other in time. Of the more descriptive passages that show the two ways working in harmony, however, M.3.135 is reasonably typical by beginning with *sati* and demonstrating how this merges with *samādhi*. Here the stages of meditational development are outlined as first equipping oneself with the resolve to practise mindfulness. This in turn permits one to abandon the harmful bonds known as the five hindrances (*pañca nīvaraṇāni*). Then there is freedom to undertake the discipline of mindfulness, a procedure which is complemented by the emergence of the *jhāna* (states of experience) which constitute meditation. Looking more carefully at this sequence and its principal components, there is a path which seems to start with the physical and volitional responsibility of attending to every waking action, no matter how commonplace. This sort of attention is both mindful and discriminatory (*satisampajañña*). Its task is the development not only of sense control and self-control through gradual purification (*parisodheti*) of the mind (*citta*), but also the development of insight into the causal undergirding of the self and the origins of impurity. Even with mindfulness then, the pattern of development shifts from the initial volitional resolve to obtain the goal to the more noetic emphasis of understanding the nature of that goal. It is at this point that meditation can be of help to mindfulness by providing the equilibrium and calm needed to sustain the vision, the insight that leads to salvation. It is as if *sati* spills over into *samādhi*, although it should be emphasized that the latter only reinforces the former.

The term *samādhi* now has to be further refined. A
key text (A.4.448) avers that there are traditionally
nine (*nava*) gradually ascending stages of consciousness
(*anupubbavihārā* or *jhānā*). The Pāli Text Society dictionary indicates that these nine stages are in turn
grouped into three units. First, there are the four
so-called *rūpa jhānā* (absorptions or states of consciousness with "form"); then four *arūpa jhānā* ("formless"
absorptions); and, finally, "the crowning phase" of
saññāvedayitanirodha or the "complete cessation of
perception and feeling."

The important difference between meditation (*samādhi*)
and mindfulness (*sati*) is that the *jhānā* which make up
samādhi are unique one-pointed "non-natural" states of
mind which resist external influence. The kind of
knowledge that emerges from them differs from the more
cerebral epistemic foundation of ordinary states of
consciousness. This interpretation is consistent with
what the Pāli Text Society dictionary observes about
jhāna when it comments that, although the word literally
implies meditation, "it never means vaguely meditation,
[but] is the technical term for a special religious
experience, reached in a certain order of mental
states."[34] As was briefly noted in Chapter Two, the
jhānā are usually identified with specific characteristics
present in any one of several particular states. Thus
in S.2.210, the first *jhāna* is known as joy and happiness
arising from detachment (*vivekaja pītisukha*), the second
as inner tranquillity (*ajjhatta sampasādana*), the third
as attentive mind (*sampajāna*), and the fourth as pure
neutrality (*upekkhā*). As the various states proceed
one from the other in sequence, characteristics of
previous states are eliminated, and the "religious
experience" referred to above becomes increasingly refined. Once beyond the first four stages the meditator
can enter into even more refined levels, the so-called
"formless" *arūpa jhānā*, sometimes also known as the
āyatanāni or "spheres of the series." These are identified as the sphere of infinite space (*ākāsānañcāyatana*),

the sphere of unbounded consciousness (*viññāṇānañcāyatana*) the sphere of infinite consciousness (*ākiñcaññāyatana*), the sphere of neither perception nor non-perception (*nevasaññānāsaññāyatana*). Ninth and finally, in some texts there is reference to the cessation of all perception and feeling (*saññāvedayitanirodha*).

Although it may be confusing to the reader of the Pāli texts, it should be noted that sometimes the list of the first four *jhānā* is expressed differently (D.2.112), and the fourth state of neutrality (*upekkhā*) will be by-passed. The meditator is said to enter directly into the level identified above as "the sphere of infinite space" (*ākāsānañcāyatana*). This means, of course, that in such a chronology there will be eight, rather than nine, levels of "religious experience." I do not see this as a serious discrepancy, and it should be regarded merely as a variation of the one central theme of transcendence.

What indeed occurs at the final stage of *samādhi*? Some, such as Conze, maintain that we do not really know, because the texts themselves are so unclear on this matter.[35] There is obviously an intuitive quality here that is beyond linguistic description, yet it is possible to go further and point out how both text and the living tradition suggest that consciousness (*viññāṇa*) has disappeared. *Citta* ("mind") alone experiences the freedom from emotion (D.2.81), serenity (S.1.76), calm (D.1.71), and destruction of the deep-rooted cankers (*āsavā*, S.3.45), identified with this noble state.

Although this is at times referred to as the "final" or *nirodha* (cessation) level, it must not be confused with wisdom (*paññā*), or nirvāṇa; for, as T. W. Rhys Davids points out,

> The *jhānas* are only a means, not an end. To imagine that experiencing them was equivalent to Arahantship (and was therefore the end aimed at) is condemned (D.1.37) as a deadly heresy.... It was because they made

> this the aim of their teaching that Gotama rejected the doctrines of his two teachers, Āḷāra-Kāḷāma and Uddaka-Rāmaputta (M.1.164).[36]

Others have argued that although the final state is mainly "emptiness," it is still invested with intellectual clarity. In other words, it is still "an act of knowledge or conviction," something just short of nirvāṇa itself.[37]

Thus nirvāṇa is not reserved for those who have achieved the highest states of *samādhi*. Not only is there the example of M.3.20, in which nirvāṇa is said to be achieved without meditation; other texts point out that the realization of nirvāṇa can be experienced at any of the levels (*jhānā*) of *samādhi*. Indeed, tradition claims that the completely emancipated Buddha himself died while only in the fourth level (D.2.156).

It is here prudent to re-emphasize the close continuity between *sati* and *samādhi*. Although *sati* is clearly the more important of the two procedures of meditation, *samādhi* can obviously assist in its advancement. Apart from preparing the mindful one for achievement in "insight knowledge" (*vipassanā*) through the cultivation of calmness and neutralization of craving, *samādhi* also reinforces awareness and acceptance of impermanency. A good example of this relation is found in M.1.435, where the two procedures are truly combined:

> Here, Ananda, a monk, by detachment from the basis of rebirth (*upadhivivekā*), by getting rid of unskilled states of mind (*akusalānaṃ dhammānaṃ*), by abandoning every corruption of the body, detached from sense pleasures, detached from unskilled states of mind, enters and abides in the first *jhāna* which is accompanied by initial and discursive thought, is born of detachment, and is joyful. Whatever is there of form, feeling, ideation, activity, he looks on these as impermanent, painful, a disease, a boil, a dart, a misfortune, an affliction, as something apart, as decay, empty, not-self. He turns his mind from these things and when he has done so he focusses his mind on the

> deathless element (*amatāya dhātuyā*), thinking: this is the real (*santaṃ*), this is the excellent, that is to say the tranquillizing of all activities, the removal of all clinging, the destruction of craving; it is dispassion, stopping, nirvāṇa. M.1.435

Although the classical tradition allows for and even encourages the joint pursuit of *sati* and *samādhi* by the meditator, this is not commonly found in contemporary practice.[38] *Samādhi* needs time, more often than not a great deal of it, and most life-styles in the modern Theravāda world cannot adequately provide for this. In many ways, then, *samādhi* has become a monastic pursuit. *Sati* or *vipassanā*, on the other hand, is less demanding and more meaningful, and available to the average person. Today many meditation centres and teachers in South and Southeast Asia focus primarily upon *sati* techniques. In the long run these techniques should be consistent with the practice indicated in the Satipaṭṭhāna Sutta, but there are some very real differences in approach. In Sri Lanka, for instance, Nyanaponika is representative of a widespread attitude to *sati* when he urges the observance of an historically later aspect of it known as "bare attention" (*sukkha vipassanā*). Although this term does not occur in the Sutta Piṭaka there are numerous passages in the texts that reflect this method. Basically it is just "the clear and single-minded awareness of what actually happens to us and in us at the successive moments of perception."[39] It differs little from the central aim of *sati* first laid down by the Buddha. This is likewise frequently encountered in Thailand and Burma, with sometimes interesting alterations or modifications, depending on the school. So, for example, Dhammasudhi of Thailand teaches "passive watchfulness" as the key to *sati*,[40] letting the breathing process come and go "naturally and normally," with no overt "desire to achieve." How different this is from the fiercely aggressive method of Sunlungukyaung Sayadaw of Burma.

Although this master died in 1952, his procedure is practised and respected in many parts of Burma. Sunlun presses on to the eradication of egocentricity with "burning zeal and indefatigable energy." "Impatient with gradualist and indirect approaches," as King reports, it reckons that the average meditator has "neither the time nor energy for acquiring *jhānic* skills."[41] Consequently the method enjoins concentrated intensity and "rough breathing" to pursue the central aim of mindfulness. This is a departure from the traditional practices found elsewhere.

It is not to be thought that the practice of meditation has fallen away with the advent of modernization in South and Southeast Asia, or that it is confined to the monastic quest for perfection. But in this regard, it should be noted that meditation of any kind is more widespread in Burma than in Sri Lanka or Thailand, even amongst the clergy. I know of many monks in Lanka, for instance, who do not systematically meditate, and some who do not meditate at all. In Burma, however, one cannot avoid being aware of the prominence of meditation in daily life, even amongst lay devotees. Is this so because the Burmese *sangha* is traditionally open to males for a short period of religious vocation, and therefore the practice of meditation becomes a life discipline? The same custom of a spell of religious vocation is also prevalent and respected in Thailand, but there meditation is only a little more pursued than it is in Sri Lanka.

The tradition of meditation in Burma has not succumbed to the forces of modernity in the way it has in Sri Lanka and Thailand. It still lends itself very much to the Burmese way of life and outlook.

It seems clear that meditation is the traditional, accepted Buddhist procedure for coming to grips with egocentricity and craving. Contemporary devotees, to be sure, now as before, know that mindfulness and meditation by themselves are not salvation. They only prepare one for wisdom (*paññā*) and nirvāṇa. But what for the Buddhist does this wisdom imply?

8. Wisdom (*Paññā*) and Nirvāṇa

It is *paññā* (wisdom, insight) and not meditation which is the real crisis of religious experience in Buddhism. The central question,however, is the nature of this insight. What final truth or truths does wisdom impart? *Paññā* as realization or pure thought is an understanding that goes beyond the range of ordinary empirical knowledge (*ñāṇa*). One of the limitations of commonsense, everyday knowledge, is that, although it contributes to salvation, it still does not free one from "*upadhika*" (literally "having a substratum," "showing attachment to rebirth"). Sn. 789 points out:

> If one's purification (*suddhi*) is by seeing (*diṭṭhena*), and he gives up painfulness by ordinary knowledge (*ñaṇena*), he becomes pure in a different way (i.e., from the way of *paññā*), being still "attached to rebirth."

At this point controversy arises. Granting that *paññā* is more than ordinary knowledge, how much does it differ from the method of deduction and analysis which operates in ordinary knowledge? In other words, is *paññā* a sort of experience which has some relation to ordinary knowledge, or is it wholly metaphysical in nature, having a mystical and unfathomable spiritual character? Is it part of a progression to insight that has as its beginning intellectual understanding and culminates in an experience at least partially based on that kind of understanding? There is support for both points of view.

A metaphysical definition of *paññā* is favoured chiefly by A. B. Keith,[42] C. A. Moore,[43] E. Conze,[44] and H. D. Lewis.[45] Keith made the first radical defence of an enlightenment based totally on a non-empirical theory of knowledge when he wrote:

> The place available for reasoning is limited, in that, although the Buddha in the Suttas reasoned and instructed by analogy and parable and simple deductive argument, it is not claimed

> that he attained his saving insight by this means and still less that the insight itself consists of any such reasoning: the Buddha attained his enlightenment in complete intuition, the fruit of a long process in which he overcame all forms of empirical knowledge.[46]

Keith's argument is largely supported by C. A. Moore, who treats the question of the nature of enlightenment as only a part of the much larger difficulty Buddhism has with the limitations of scientific method. Moore's case is built on an extensive attack directed against those who argue for an intimate affinity or compatability between Buddhism and the methods of science. It is along these lines that Conze writes about "the mystery of enlightenment,"[47] for he too rejects models of comparison that attempt to tie the goal and methods of meditation with, for example, the scientific aims and procedure of psychotherapy.

Others scholars object to a view of enlightenment grounded on anything but an intuitive insight because they take that experience to be ineffable. A good example is H. D. Lewis, who writes that "the illumination which the Buddha claimed...falls into an entirely different class from the normal discovery of truth at the scientific or philosophic level. It has more in common with the raptures of the artist."[48]

The most serious criticism of this approach is that it discourages discussion on the nature of enlightenment. And yet, as Radhakrishnan says, even though it is difficult to express the truths of the experience of enlightenment, we cannot be content with saying that the experience is ineffable,[49] no matter what the obstacles to communicating it are, if any religious sense is to be made of that experience.

The other side of the issue is argued forcefully by G. P. Malalasekera,[50] C. Humphreys,[51] A. K. Warder,[52] R. Johansson,[53] and above all K. N. Jayatilleke.[54] Chapter Two expressed agreement with Jayatilleke's account of the Buddhist theory of knowledge and developed its essential points. Jayatilleke and others are critical about capricious use of the word "intuition." Moore, for instance, engages an argument which contains only a few undocumented references to the Sutta Piṭaka, and not a single word of Pāli. He talks loosely of "intuitive insight." The careful reader is led to ask what he means by intuition and how it is different from other forms of knowledge. As Jayatilleke has shown, the term intuition in Pāli is variously translated as *jānāti*, *abhiññā paññā*, and *ñāṇa*,[55] each with a different connotation in varying contexts.

In fairness to Keith, he refers only to *paññā* as intuition. But his assertion that "like the sage in the Upaniṣads" the Buddha's insight is also an intuition of "mystical potency" is vulnerable to Jayatilleke's refutation by better use of the Pāli texts. Thus Jayatilleke writes:

> In the Upaniṣads one's knowledge and vision is not, in the final analysis, due to one's efforts but to the grace or intervention of Ātman or God. The emergence of this knowledge is conceived as something inexplicable and mysterious. This character warrants it being called a kind of mystical knowledge. But in the Buddhist account the mental concentration (*samādhi*) which is a product of training and effort, is a causal factor (*upanisā*) in the production of this knowledge (A.3.200; 5.313).... Here "knowledge and insight" (*ñāṇadassana*) which is a means to an end and is often called *paññā* as well as the final "knowledge and insight of emancipation" (*vimuttiñāṇadassana*) which is the end itself, are considered to be natural occurrences.... His enlightenment [therefore] is not considered to be a mysterious single act of intuition, but the discovery by means of the developed natural faculties of the mind of the cause and cessation of suffering.[56]

From the context of Jayatilleke's criticisms, it is clear that one of his central aims is to refute any suggestion that *paññā* is an experience of a sort of other-worldly "truth." He does not say that it is only an intellectual insight into "the knowledge and insight of things as they are" (*yathābhūtañāṇadassana*). It may in part be this (S.2.30; 5.432), but it is also the "knowledge and vision of salvation" (*vimuttiñāṇadassana* M.1.145, A.3.81). "Salvation," however, is not to be taken as an abstract metaphysical truth. It may have become just this to later Buddhism, but it was not so in the Sutta Piṭaka.

How do the texts describe *paññā*? They refer to it as an experience of understanding based on realization, learning, and practice (*cintā-mayā paññā*, *suta-mayā paññā*, *bhāvanā-mayā paññā*, D.3.219). Secondly, as has been shown, they recognize the crucial element of introspection (*vipassanā*) in the meaning and validity of the great truths taught by the Buddha. This insight is not established by transcendental or metaphysical revelation. It is an experiential encounter with reality that is best described in terms of seeing through a veil of ignorance and craving, or of "seeing" the four Noble Truths, just as M.1.280 tells us one sees through the surface of a pool of water to detect "oysters and shells, gravel and pebbles, and shoals of fish moving about." So (*evaṃ eva*) the aware one understands painfulness as it really is (*dukkham-ti yathābhūtaṃ pajānāti*). When he knows this (*pajānāti*) he is at once freed from the cankers (*āsavā*) and from future rebirth.

Johansson regards this passage as one of strategic significance in defining how wisdom (*paññā*) operates. He observes that:

> This is a very concrete description of the process involved: a man sees a scene and then makes a conscious reflection by means of which he understands the meaning of everything he sees; this is an act of *paññā*. In the same way, he can by introspection see himself, how he is caught in a vicious circle of causality, how everything in his life is caused and only leads to suffering, further exactly what those causes are and how the law can be used to counteract the effects—and we can understand how this vision and understanding can lead to an experience of liberation. Even dynamic

> factors (desires, emotions) may be influenced, diverted or dissolved, by a causal analysis of their origin and their effects.[57]

To sum up, *paññā* sees the true nature of reality with an experience that is far more profound than seeing painfulness, ignorance, or craving through ordinary knowledge (*ñāṇa*), even although it is causally related to that kind of knowledge. Wisdom proceeds beyond the skin of things, penetrating the genesis of becoming, providing the individual with more than just a general understanding of how ignorance and craving block insight into the momentariness of the phenomenal world. It constitutes a whole "diagnosis of spiritual illness," to use the language of Caroline Rhys Davids.[58]

The coming of wisdom gives the seeker the understanding that release from painfulness is achieved only through the proper cultivation of ethics, intention, and meditation. Through them one knows how to "change the current of desire" and how at last to dissolve that current altogether. This is nirvāṇa. Taken in this conative and ethical sense, the term can be translated as "extinction." But, as Slater cautions, this does not mean annihilation in nirvāṇa, for "it is not the possibility of life which is negated but the destructive fires (lust, ill-will and stupidity) which hinder this possibility."[59]

In nirvāṇa, the seeker is fully awake to the implications of unwholesome and misguided craving. Craving is seen not just as a particular kind of desire but as a whole mental state, conscious and unconscious, which obstructs the development of selflessness. Nirvāṇa is more than a psychological affair referring to craving as a state of mental disequilibrium. The aware one looks beyond this approach and interprets the experience of craving in a religious framework:

> Whoever sees this as it really is by perfect understanding, his craving for becoming disappears.... By the complete extinction of craving there is dispassion, cessation without remainder, nirvāṇa.
>
> *Evam etaṃ yathābhūtaṃ sammapaññāya passato bhavataṇhā pahīyati...sabbato taṇhānaṃ khayā asesavirāganirodho nibbāṇaṃ.* Ud. 33

CONCLUSION

This monograph has argued that a study of the concept of craving is crucial to an understanding of Buddhism. A psychological picture has emerged which indicates why and how craving is the central obstacle that prevents the achievement of a state of mental integrity unsoiled by egoistic and grasping aims, and therefore free from pain. In many ways this picture appears to be straightforward. But, as has been demonstrated, behind outward simplicity there is an intricate path to salvation in which craving is firmly embedded.

Once craving is examined from the perspective of salvation it is possible to recognize where the key emphases of the doctrine lie. For one, Buddhism emphasizes that craving is a persistent feature of all experience and, in turn, that it is rooted in a complex state within man, who must come to see that life is painfulness. In this way Buddhism is from the beginning importantly different from other religions. Here the problem is not taken to be a cosmic crisis nor a spiritual condition in the grip of external or daemonic forces. Nor is the pain and fault of the human condition attributed to a single part of man's nature, such as an enslaved will, confused intellect, or disoriented emotion. There is rather a permeating stain, profound and intricate, which eludes recognition. Buddhism seeks to confront and master this obstacle.

A second emphasis that emerges is the intimacy between the reality of craving and what the Buddhist understands as mind. The Buddha teaches that mind is tangled in a web of conditioning factors, the most strategic of which is craving, and that men everywhere are born into this state. An acknowledgment and definition of mind and the various factors which condition it are therefore essential for the way to salvation. The Buddha traces out the problem of craving through the various regions of the mind. In this way he shows how the mind in its conscious and unconscious operations is strategic to the arising and expression of craving.

A third emphasis comes to focus as we realize that the mind is not merely the receptacle of craving but is also the means for liberation from craving. That the mind is the context in which this whole drama of life and salvation is worked out is central to the teachings of Buddhism. The mind is regarded as corruptible but capable of correction. The Buddha teaches that it is like a lotus, born in mud and slime, often submerged beneath the defiling (*upalitta*) waters of ignorance and craving, yet at the same time it is of capable of growing and rising above these waters, a symbol of purity and enlightenment (D.2.38).

This is further reflected in the Buddha's doctrine of confidence (*visārada*), which recognizes the need for self-effort without reliance on any external agency or power. The positive nature of this teaching is apparent even in his first sermon (S.5.420) in which he lays down the path between asceticism and indulgence. Here he points to the psychological truth that coarse desires are only aggravated by a forced or unwilling effort to eradicate them. The Buddhist perspective on life is comprehensive and balanced, not a way by a mere denial or renunciation, but by inclusion and re-orientation. Even painfulness might be said to have some good in it, leading as it can to authentic religious experience (*hiri-ottappa*—shame or fear of sin). So too, craving is taken to be a factor that can be brought to balance itself. The evident need is not to repress the desires that possess the individual but to root out their origins, to understand their conditioned background, and finally to redirect this unwholesome craving to more purified aims, until at the last craving of any kind is overcome (M.1.119). In doing so, the aware one comes to the understanding that we need no longer be tethered by the leash of craving (*taṇhā gaddūla*) to a selfish and chaotic emotional life.

This understanding is confirmed and strengthened through the discipline of meditation. At this point the path toward nirvāṇa shifts from a conative to a noetic focus. Insight into the complex nature of craving is more readily achieved. It should be pointed out, however, that although even in meditation the mind is not looked upon as something mystical and otherworldly, it would be wrong to interpret the Buddhist path as only a system of mental healing and peace of mind. There is a transcendent dimension in the experience of enlightenment, an awareness not only of the sheer scope and depth of craving but of how in its deleterious form it above all contributes to that wrongness from which Buddhism invites escape.

Buddhism has sometimes been interpreted as pure mystery and sometimes as pure common sense. A study of craving demonstrates that both views are incorrect. Rather, craving is a spiritual sickness which is overcome only when, along with painfulness, it has been resolved in nirvāṇa. On the other hand, craving is a natural part of man's experience and is tackled properly only by the will and intellect of man himself. So understood, craving comes to be seen as part of a soteriological system which is practical and realistic, and yet points to ultimate resolution. This teaching is as pertinent today as it has been in the past.[1]

NOTES

INTRODUCTION

1. *"Akusalaṃ...pajahatha. Sakkā...akusalaṃ pajahituṃ. No ce taṃ...sakkā abhavissa akusalaṃ pajahituṃ nāhaṃ evaṃ vadeyyaṃ."* A.1.58.
2. Rune Johansson, The Psychology Of Nirvana (London: Allen, Unwin, 1969); Winston King, Theravāda Meditation (Philadelphia: Pennsylvania University Press, 1980); Padmasiri de Silva, An Introduction to Buddhist Psychology (London: Macmillan Press, 1979).
3. Robert Ornstein, The Psychology of Consciousness (New York: Viking Press, 1972); Herbert Fingarette, The Self and Transformation (New York: Basic Books, 1963); John Dunne, The Way of All the Earth (New York: Macmillan Press, 1972).
4. Soteriology means a doctrine of salvation. Although frequently found in a specifically Christian context, it is not a term confined only to that religion. G. Kittel (Theologisches Wörterbuch zum Neuen Testament, Vol. 7, trans. by G. W. Bromiley, Grand Rapids: W. B. Eerdmans, 1971, 965f) points out that *soter* and *soteria* were common words in the Attic Greek (pre-Christian) world. They had the general meaning of saving, benefitting, and preserving. H. Liddell and R. Scott (Greek-English Lexicon, New York: Harper Co., 1855, 1462) also demonstrate many non-Christian applications of the term *soteria*. Soteriology has a definite religious focus then, and can be legitimately used to describe questions related to freedom or salvation in any religious tradition. It is in this sense that I apply the word to Buddhism.
5. The textual references are limited largely to the five Nikāyas or "collections" of the Sutta Piṭaka.

This is so chiefly because the Sutta represents the central literary work of classical Buddhism, and most of its material comes from the same oral tradition associated with the earliest rehearsals of doctrine. Of the other two Piṭakas, the Vinaya and the Abhidhamma, I have made much less use. The Vinaya is for the most part concerned with rules governing the brotherhood of monks (*sangha*), and I refer to it sparingly because of this. The Abhidhamma is even more problematic because its expanded doctrine represents later, fine doctrinal distinctions. See A. K. Warder, Indian Buddhism (Varanasi: Motilal Banarsidass, 1970, 224), for an outstanding example of how the Abhidhamma has changed the focus of one of the central concepts in early Buddhism, the doctrine of causality.

6. In the context of Western thought this might, with careful qualification, be termed "theological." Such an interpretation of the word "theology" is perhaps best stated by Paul Tillich, who defines theological problems as those that lie at the heart of any religion. Thus he writes that theology deals primarily with questions of "ultimate concern" and, further, that "the 'situation' to which theology must respond is the totality of man's creative self-interpretation in a special period" (Systematic Theology, Vol. 1, Chicago: University of Chicago Press, 1951), 4, 21f. For some, this may not, sensu stricto, be applied to Theravāda Buddhism.

Chapter 1: CRAVING AND PAINFULNESS

1. "Thus spoke the Blessed One. Delighted, the monks rejoiced in what he said. And while this exposition was being spoken, the minds of as many as sixty monks were freed from the mental cankers with no grasping lift."
"Idam avoca Bhagavā. Attamanā te bhikkhū Bhagavato bhāsitaṃ abhinandun ti. Imasmiṃ kho pana veyyā-

karanasmim bhaññamāne satthimattānam bhikkhūnam anupādāya āsavehi cittāni vimuccimsūti." M.3.20.

2. T. W. Rhys-Davids, Pali-English Dictionary (London: Luzac, 1966), 324.
3. V. F. Gunaratne, The Significance of the Four Noble Truths (Kandy: B.P.S., 1968), 8.
4. Some prefer to interpret *sankhāra dukkhatā* as the suffering that results from sensing the instability of all "conditioned states" that make up the individual (see The Book of the Kindred Sayings III, trans. by F. L. Woodward, London: Luzac, 1954, 72). But as K. N. Jayatilleke convincingly argues, if *sankhāra* here refers only to "component things," then it would really be identical to *viparināma dukkha*. Rather, he points out, *sankhāra* should mean "purposive psychological activities" to indicate subjective as well as objective transiency. ("Some problems of Translation and Interpretation," University of Ceylon Review 7 (1949), 218).
5. A comparison of the Maitrī Upanisad 1.3 and M.1.130 shows almost identical concern with the momentary condition of mortal life.
6. Although I am here chiefly interested in seeing the problem of painfulness from the perspective of craving and the second noble truth, controversy arises as to whether the second truth does in fact adequately express the full range of *dukkha*. In this regard, Paul Younger is right when he notes that "traditionally there have been two somewhat different lines of interpretation, depending on whether one saw the second or the third Truth as the key to the interpretation of the first. Those who saw the second Truth as the key to this theological system tended to interpret *duhkha* primarily in psychological terms, as a description of the experienced reality of the world. On the other hand, those who saw the third Truth as the key tended to interpret *duhkha* in philosophical terms as the way of speaking about a world which is essentially an unreal distortion of

the Ideal or *Nirvāṇa*" (The Indian Religious Tradition, Varanasi: Bharatiya Vidya Prakashan, 1970, 39). This basic difference in approach reflects the two great historical branches of Buddhism, with the Theravāda opting for an interpretation of painfulness as disequilibrium and ignorance and the Mahāyāna proposing something more metaphysical, a state of bondage to the "play of phenomena," to use T. R. V. Murti's words, "with no recognition of the noumenal unconditioned reality which lies behind" (The Central Philosophy of Buddhism, London: Allen, Unwin, 1968, 258).

7. *"Sakkāyo sakkāyo ti ayye vuccati. Katamo nu kho ayye sakkāyo vutto Bhagavatā ti?"* M.1.299.

8. See S.4.196, the parable of the *vīṇā*, where the mellifluous sound of this instrument so intrigued a certain king that he sought unsuccessfully to find its source by breaking the instrument up into small parts. Likewise in S.1.135, the parable of the chariot, which is shown to be a vehicle only when all of its parts are together. In a like manner, a human "being" is acknowledged in a conventional way when the human factors are all present. Concerning the question of the two levels of understanding or truth (*sacca*), Jayatilleke rightly points out that this distinction is only to be inferred from the Pāli Tipiṭika. It is not carefully worked out until the later commentarial literature (viz. Manorathapūraṇī 2.118). See Early Buddhist Theory of Knowledge (London: Allen, Unwin, 1963), 361. A good discussion of the two levels of acknowledgment of the doctrine of self is found in Steven Collins, Selfless Persons (London: Cambridge University Press, 1982), Part III.

9. Rune Johansson rightly prefers to call them "building complexes." The Dynamic Psychology of Early Buddhism (Oxford: Curzon Press, 1979), 67.

10. E. R. Saratchandra, The Buddhist Psychology of Perception (Colombo: Associated Newspapers of

Ceylon, 1958), 103.

11. S. S. Tomkins, Affect, Imagery, Consciousness, Vol. 2 (New York: Springer, 1965), 157.
12. Jayatilleke, "Some Problems of Translation and Interpretation," 233.
13. *"Samudayo samudayo ti kho me bhikkhave pubbe ananussutesu dhammesu cakkhum udapādi ñāṇam udapādi paññā udapādi vijjā udapādi āloko udapādi."* S.2.10
14. A. B. Keith, Buddhist Philosophy (Varanasi: Chowkhamba Series, 1963), 113; C. J. Thomas, The Life of the Buddha as Legend and History (London: Kegan Paul, 1927), 199; R. E. Hume, "Miracles in the Canonical Scriptures of Buddhism," Journal of the American Oriental Society, 44 (1927), 162.
15. G. Grimm, The Doctrine of the Buddha (Delhi: Motilal Banarsidass, 1973), 175.
16. Introduction to the Mahānidānasutta (D.2.55), Dialogues of the Buddha, Vol. 2 (London: Luzac), 42f.
17. Jayatilleke, Early Buddhist Theory of Knowledge, 451.
18. Johansson is probably right when he points out that here ignorance does not so much "cause" the other factors as "permit" them to continue. In this way he equates it with certain "natural impulses." The Dynamic Psychology of Early Buddhism, 133.
19. This is suggested in the parable of the seamstress: "Impression (or contact) monks, is the first end, its arising is the second, its ceasing is in the middle, and craving is the seamstress; for craving sews a man to this rebirth and becoming." *"Phasso kho bhikkhave eko anto, phassasamudayo dutiyo anto, phassanirodho majjhe, taṇhā sibbanī; taṇhā hi naṃ sibbati tassa tass 'eva bhavassa abhinibbattiyā.'"* A.3.401.
20. Lama Govinda emphasizes how the Buddhist sense of birth (*jāti*) is more than the physical moment of being born into this world, but it is as well the on-going process of "conceiving" that is "called forth continually through the senses." So understood, we are constantly being "reborn" in our daily

physiological and mental activity. See *The Psychological Attitude of Early Buddhist Philosophy* (London: Rider Press, 1961), 50.

21. Johansson, *The Psychology of Nirvana*, 66.

Chapter 2: MIND AND CRAVING

1. Bhikkhu Ñāṇananda gives a good discussion of *papañca* in this context as "conceptual proliferation." See *Concept and Reality in Early Buddhist Thought* (Kandy: B.P.S., 1971), 5.
2. Although *saññā* (perception) is strictly speaking not listed as one of the traditional spokes in the Series of Dependencies, its function is taken for granted in the factors of *saḷāyatana* (six sense bases) and *phasso* (contact).
3. E. R. Saratchandra, *The Buddhist Psychology of Perception* (Colombo: Associated Newspapers of Ceylon, 1958), 10.
4. K. N. Jayatilleke, *Early Buddhist Theory of Knowledge* (London: Allen, Unwin, 1963), 434.
5. Rune Johansson, *The Psychology of Nirvana* (London: Allen, Unwin, 1969), 80.
6. "Consciousness (*viññāṇa*) is firmly supported by means of perception (*saññā*); with perception as object, with perception as support, it attains to happiness, growth, increase, and full development." D.3.228.
7. Johansson, *Psychology of Nirvana*, 82.
8. Sati, a follower of the teachings (*dhamma*), apparently thought that consciousness transmigrates without change of identity: "Your reverences, even so do I understand that *dhamma* taught by the Blessed One, that it is this consciousness itself that runs on, fares on, not another".
(Evaṃ byā kho ahaṃ āvuso Bhagavatā dhammaṃ desitaṃ ājānāmi yathā tad ev'idaṃ viññāṇaṃ sandhāvati saṃsarati, anaññan-ti) M.1.256.
9. See G. P. Malalasekera, who writes of the "subterranean flow of energies" which come from the

past but have a significance extending into the future. "Some Aspects of Buddhism," in S. Yamaguchi, ed., Buddhism and Culture (Kyoto: Nakana Press, 1960), 65.

10. Notes Saratchandra: "It was for him not a topic of prime importance. What was important was to realize that our normal empirical consciousness was not a stable entity as the philosophers of the time were trying to make out.... The question as to what part of the individual actually survived through his various births would naturally arise in the popular mind, since the Buddha had not refuted the prevalent belief in reincarnation," Buddhist Psychology of Perception, 10.

11. Jayatilleke, Early Buddhist Theory of Knowledge, 374; "The Buddhist View of Survival" in Survival and Karma (Kandy: B.P.S. 1969), 2,8f.

12. O. H. de Wijesekera, "The Concept of *Viññāṇa* in Theravāda Buddhism," Journal of the American Oriental Society 84 (1964), 254.

13. "At the breaking up of the body after dying this situation exists, that the evolving consciousness may accordingly reach imperturbability." *"Kāyassa bhedā param maraṇā ṭhānam etaṃ vijjati yaṃ taṃ saṃvattanikaṃ viññāṇaṃ assa āṇañjūpagaṃ....* M.2.262. (I. B. Horner's translation, Middle Length Sayings III, [London: Luzac, 1959], 47).

14. *Kamma* (Pāli, from the Sanskrit *karma*—action, deed) is best defined in the Cūḷakammavibhaṅga Sutta and the Mahākammavibhaṅga Sutta (M.3.203f.), where we are provided with a reliable explanation of how it operates. Here the function of *kamma* is defined in terms of volitional actions, good (*kusala*, literally "skillful"), bad (*akusala*), or neutral (*avyākata*). As "actions," they may refer to bodily behaviour (*kāyakamma*), verbal behaviour (*vacīkamma*), and psychological behaviour (*manokamma*). But central to the doctrine of *kamma* is the intentional, conscious volition (*cetanā*) that stands behind

behaviour or action. The volitional dimension of *kamma* is what gives it its soteriological significance in Buddhism: "Venerable Samiddhi, when one has intentionally done a deed by body, speech or thought, what does one experience? When one has intentionally done a deed by body, speech or thought, friend Potali's son, one experiences painfulness."
(*"Sañcetanikaṃ āvuso Samiddhi, kammaṃ katvā kāyena vācāya manasā, kiṃ so vediyatīti? Sañcetanikaṃ āvuso Potaliputta, kammaṃ katvā kāyena vācāya manasā, dukkhaṃ so vediyatīti."*) M.3.207

15. Cited by V. F. Gunaratne, Rebirth Explained (Kandy: B.P.S., 1971), 14; and Johansson, Psychology of Nirvana, 81.
16. *"Seyyathāpi...aggi sa-upādāno jalati no-anupādāno, evaṃ ave khvāhaṃ...sa-upādānassa upapattiṃ paññāpemi no anupādānassa ti...samaye imañ ca kāyaṃ nikkhipati satto ca aññataraṃ kāyaṃ anuppanno hoti...taṃ ahaṃ taṇhupādānaṃ vadāmi; taṇhā hissa...tasmiṃ samaye upādānaṃ hotī tī..."* S.4.399.
17. *"Yaṃ ca kho etaṃ bhikkhave vuccati cittaṃ iti pi mano iti pi viññāṇaṃ iti pi, tatrassutavā puthujjano nālaṃ nibbindituṃ nālaṃ virajjituṃ nalaṃ vimuccituṃ. Taṃ kissa hetu? Dīgharattaṃ hetaṃ bhikkhave assutavato puthujjanassa ajjhositaṃ mamāyitaṃ parāmaṭṭhaṃ: Etaṃ mama eso haṃ asmi eso me attāti."* S.2.94.
18. Bṛhad-āraṇyaka Upaniṣad 1.3.6. As well, see Chāndogya Upaniṣad 6.6.2 for Uddālaka's materialist concept of *manas*.
19. *"Manomayo 'yaṃ puruṣaḥ...sa eṣa sarvasyeśānaḥ"* —"This person consisting of mind...is lord of all." Bṛhad-āraṇyaka Upaniṣad 5.6.1.
20. E. J. Thomas, The History of Buddhist Thought (London: Routledge, Kegan, Paul, 1969), 77.
21. R. G. Wettimuny, The Buddha's Teaching (Colombo: M. D. Gunasena, 1969), 167.

22. *"Imesaṃ kho...pañcannaṃ indriyānaṃ nānāvisayānaṃ nānāgocarānam na aññamaññassa gocaravisayaṃ paccanubhontānaṃ mano paṭisaraṇaṃ, mano ca nesaṃ gocaravisayaṃ paccanubhotīti."*
23. Johansson remarks that *mano* could also refer here to "a day-dreaming function or to emotional attachment." "A Psychosomatic Investigation," University of Ceylon Review 23 (1969), 186. It should be pointed out that in this exceptional, indeed seminal, article, Johansson set down what was really the first modern analysis of psychological terminology in the Sutta Piṭaka. He thus found it unnecessary to use later Abhidhamma Piṭaka sources, and suggested that reliable and sufficient material is to be found in the earlier scriptures. I am indebted to him for pointing out several interesting texts, especially from the Saṃyutta Nikaya.
24. A common feature of the Abhidhamma Piṭaka is that *citta* is depicted as almost a kind of "self" around which everything else is arranged. This concept is frequently found in diagrams designed to explain the Abhidhamma position. See H. V. Guenther, Philosophy and Psychology in the Abhidhamma (Lucknow: Pioneer Press, 1956), 22, for a good example.
25. Johansson, Psychology of Nirvana, 61.
26. Johannson, "A Psychosomatic Investigation," 210.
27. Ibid., 212.
28. Johansson, Psychology of Nirvana, 83.
29. Aside from sharing the same root, *citta* and *ceto* share many similar aspects. Some of these directly involve descriptions of the "impure mind" (*cetaso upakkilese*, D.3.49; *cittassa upakkilesā*, S.5.92, 108, 115) and of efforts to purify if (*parisuddhena cetasā*, M.3.94; *citte parisuddhe*, D.1.76) through meditation (*cetosamādhiṃ*, M.3.108; *cittasamādhiṃ*, S.4.350). As a synonym for *citta*, *ceto* is also employed as meaning the mental factor which attains "freedom" (*vimutti*) at different *jhānic* or

meditational stages, an important feature pointed out in M.1.297.

30. Perhaps this difficulty provokes Johansson to write that "the vague term 'mind' may, after all, be the best translation, although it does not cover the emotional and moral aspects." "A Psychosomatic Investigation," 178.

31. See Johansson, Dynamic Psychology of Early Buddhism, 157f.

32. See Aloysius Peiris, who writes "more accurately, *mano*, *citta* and *viññāṇa* are three different ways of viewing the same reality," even though this fact is "not formally stated anywhere in Pāli literature." "The Notions of *Citta*, *Attā* and *Attabhāva* in the Pāli Exegetical Writings," Pāli Buddhist Review 4, No. 2 (1979), 5. Also, Walpola Rahula, who remarks that in both the Piṭakas and the commentaries, the three terms under discussion are considered as synonyms denoting the same thing. It was only with Asaṅga of the later Yogācāra School that the group (*khandha*) of *viññāṇa* was divided into three distinct parts or "layers." See Encyclopedia of Buddhism (Colombo: Ceylon Government Press, 1966), 5.

33. T. J. Sun, "Psychology in Primitive Buddhism," Psychoanalytic Review 11 (1924), 39.

34. The concern here is only with the activity of the unconscious as it appears in the Sutta Piṭaka. In later Buddhist literature, both in the Abhidhamma and in the Commentaries, the notion of the unconscious becomes increasingly sophisticated. Commentarial development of this idea revolves chiefly around the term *bhavaṅga*, which in turn appears to have a dual meaning: as a "life-stream" of which we are not fully conscious, or as a "life-continuum" factor. See Nyanatiloka, Buddhist Dictionary (Dondanduwa: Island Hermitage, 1956), 29; and Shwe Aung, Compendium of Philosophy (London: Luzac, 1963), 263f. This term appears only once in

the Sutta Piṭaka (A.2.79), although most scholars I have consulted about this passage, recently including U Thattila Sayadaw and U Narada Sayadaw of Rangoon, regard it as a corruption of the word *bhavagga* ("the best state of existence").

35. K. N. Jayatilleke, "Buddhism and the Scientific Revolution," in Buddhism and Science (Kandy: B.P.S., 1948).
36. Jayatilleke, "Some Problems of Translation and Interpretation," 216.
37. W. F. Jayasuriya, The Psychology and Philosophy of Buddhism (Colombo: Y.M.B.A., 1963).
38. M. W. P. de Silva, Buddhist and Freudian Psychology (Colombo: Lake House Investments, 1973), 49; and in An Introduction to Buddhist Psychology (London: Macmillan, 1979), 72.
39. Jayatilleke, "Buddhism and the Scientific Revolution," 4.
40. Cf. p. 13 above.
41. Jayatilleke directs us to Bṛhad-āranyaka Upaniṣad 4.4.5: *"Sa yathākāmo bhavati, tat kratur bhavati, yat kratur bhavati, tat karma kurute"*—"As is his desire, such in his resolve; as is his resolve, such is the action he performs." K. N. Jayatilleke's translation, "Some Problems in Translation and Interpretation," 221.
42. Pali-English Dictionary (London: Luzac, 1966), 70.
43. Dialogues of the Buddha, III (London: Luzac, 1956), translation of D.3.217.
44. Kindred Sayings, II (London: Luzac, 1952), translation of S.2.82.
45. Gradual Sayings, I (London: Luzac, 1951), translation of A.1.111.
46. Jayatilleke, "Some Problems in Translation and Interpretation," 215.
47. de Silva, An Introduction to Buddhist Psychology, 35f. In general, Chapter 3 of this text on "Motivation and Emotion" is the best single review of Buddhist motivational questions.

48. Jayatilleke, "Some Problems in Translation and Interpretation," 216.
49. Ibid., 216.
50. Ibid., 217.
51. A compilation of these lists would include the various aspects of *taṇhā* (craving) already discussed (M.1.299) as well as assorted graspings (*upādānā*, M.1.66), cankers (*āsavā*, M.1.279), hindrances (*nīvaraṇāni*, M.1.276), inclinations (*anusayā*, D.3.254), unskillful roots (*akusala-mūlā*, A.1.203), fetters (*saṃyojanāni*, A.5.17), "behaviours" (*ṭhānehi*, D.3.182), bondages of the mind (*cestaso vinibhandhā*, M.1.103), indulgences (*paṭisevanā*, M.1.10), and "floods" (*oghā*, S.1.3).
52. See Jayasuriya, who writes that the *anusayā* "may be regarded as the level of the unconscious mind of the psychologists." Psychology and Philosophy of Buddhism, 198. Johansson, notably, remains unconvinced that the *anusayā* are the same as what Freudian psychoanalysis terms the unconscious. He argues that, although they may be said to be dormant and unconscious in one sense, the Pāli texts are not clear about the influence the *anusayā* have in this state. See Dynamic Psychology of Early Buddhism, 109.
53. "That which is willed (*ceteti*), and that which is intended (*pakappeti*), and that which lies as dormant tendencies (*anuseti*), this becomes a basis (*ṭhitiyā*) for a state of consciousness (*viññāṇassa*). If the basis is there, there will be a state of consciousness .... Even if we do not will or intend, there is still a dormant tendency, and this becomes a basis for consciousness," S.2.65.
54. Although *vibhava taṇhā* is normally associated with desire for death, it can also refer to ascetic practices and, paradoxically, to the desire for power and prosperity, with the attendant aggression and ambition that accompanies such craving. See S. Radhakrishnan, The Dhammapada (Madras: Oxford

University Press, 1966), 165.

55. This is best brought out in the parable of the washerman, S.3.131. Here a stained cloth is given to a washerman (*rajaka*) who rubs it with salt-earth, lye, or cow dung, and rinses it in clear water. But although the cloth is clean, the smell of the cleansing agent remains. "Even so, friends," the passage continues, "though an Arayan disciple has put away the five lower fetters (*pañcorambhāgiyāni*), yet there remains in him from among the Five Grasping Groups a subtle remnant (*anusahagato*) of the 'I—am' (*asmīti*) conceit (*māno*), of the 'I-desire,' of the lurking tendency (*anusayo*) to think 'I am' still not removed from him."

56. Jayasuriya, Psychology and Philosophy of Buddhism, 211.

57. Pali-English Dictionary, 115.

58. I. B. Horner, Middle Length Sayings I (London: Luzac, 1967), "Discourse on all the Cankers," (Sabbāsava Sutta), 8.

59. Johansson, Dynamic Psychology of Early Buddhism, 177. He points out that the *āsavā* translated as "influxes" suggests the same as the *oghā* or "floods"; but although the "floods" are similar to the cankers, the word is rare in the older texts.

60. Sometimes, especially in the Saṃyutta Nikāya, the eradication of the unwholesome roots is compared to nirvāṇa (S.4.251), but with the understanding that these roots disappear only if the cankers are destroyed.

Chapter 3: CRAVING AND EMANCIPATION

1. H. B. and A. C. English, A Comprehensive Dictionary of Psychological and Psychoanalytical Terms (New York: Longmans, 1958): "Historically, conation was co-ordinate with cognition and affection, and was often conceived as a mental faculty. It is now seldom used for a specific form of behaviour, rather for an aspect found in all [three categories]."

2. Perhaps the most celebrated critic of this arbitrary classification of mind is Gilbert Ryle, The Concept of the Mind (Aylesbury: Penguin Books, 1968), 62f, who argues that the will is more of an "occurrence of processes or operations," and "not a Faculty, Immaterial Organ or Ministry."
3. A. Schopenhauer, The World as Will and Representation II (New York: Dover Press, 1966), 311f.
4. C. A. F. Rhys Davids, "On the Will in Buddhism," Journal of the Royal Asiatic Society 10 (1898).
5. Ibid., 54, 57. It is recognized that *visattikā* emphasizes the clinging aspect of desire, but the English word "attachment" is superior to Mrs. Rhys Davids' somewhat Victorian "dart of lust."
6. Ibid., 48.
7. Ibid., 50.
8. "The stony, stultified, self-centred apathy we often hear ascribed to the Buddhist ideal is supposed to be the result of a Schopenhauerian pessimism as to the worth and promise of life and the springs of life. If, however, the critic would dwell more on the positive tendencies in Buddhist ethics, he might discern under the outward calm or mien of the Buddhist sage in literature and art, a passion of emotion and will not paralyzed or expurgated, but rendered subservient to and diffused around deep faith and high hope," ibid., 55.
9. A Toynbee, An Historian's Approach to Religion (London: Oxford University Press, 1956), 64.
10. D. K. Swearer, Secrets of the Lotus (New York: Macmillan Press, 1971), 17.
11. D. K. Swearer, "The Appeal of Buddhism: A Christian Perspective," The Christian Century (November, 1971), 1290.
12. The Eightfold Path is traditionally organized into three parts: (i) insight (*paññā*), consisting of right understanding and thought; (ii) morality (*sīla*), representing right speech, action and livelihood; and (iii) concentration or meditation

(*samādhi*), made up of right effort, mindfulness, and comcentration. There is no evidence of a causal pattern in the format of these three parts and their sequence seems arbitrary. H. V. Guenther goes on to point out that as long as the Eightfold Path "was meant as a suggestion, no objections could be raised against such a numerical presentation, but when the import of the various 'members of the path' (*anga*) were analyzed, it became apparent that the number eight could not be kept up, though this number had been hallowed by its association with the Buddha's word," Philosophy and Psychology in the Abhidhamma (Lucknow: Pioneer Press, 1957), 304. Not unexpectedly, therefore, other lists apart from the Eightfold Path detailing factors leading to emancipation are found (viz. S.5.200). Jayatilleke reviews these carefully in his Early Buddhist Theory of Knowledge, 396.

13. *"Katamo c'āvuso sammāvāyamo. Idha...bhikkhu anuppannānaṃ pāpakānaṃ akusalānaṃ dhammānaṃ anuppādāya chandaṃ janeti vāyamati viriyaṃ ārabhati cittaṃ pagganhāti padahati."* M.3.251.

14. T. W. Rhys Davids, Dialogues of the Buddha, III, (London: Luzac, 1965), 209.

15. R. Johansson, The Dynamic Psychology of Early Buddhism (Oxford: Curzon Press, 1979), 103. With reference to another somewhat similar passage, A.4.236, where ambition, hatred, illusion, and fear are cited as motives for giving gifts to monks, Johansson remarks, "this observation that bad motives sometimes can be used for good purposes betrays an interesting insight into the intricacies of human motivation," ibid., 105.

16. E. Conze writes: "If nirvāṇa is defined as extinction, or stopping of craving, how is it that the sage is called 'prone and inclined to nirvāṇa,' and yet still does not desire it? While someone is still at a distance from nirvāṇa, he may desire it, strive and live for it.... The desire will differ

little from the kind of 'craving' normally felt for worldly things. As his eyes are gradually opened to the true features of nirvāṇa the yogin's desire will no longer be a manifestation of craving, and rather become its negation." Buddhist Thought in India (Ann Arbor: University of Michigan Press, 1967), 67.

17. K. N. Jayatilleke, Buddhism and Peace (Kandy: B.P.S., 1969), 12.

18. Over the past few years, I have aimed to test the acceptability of this reading in the living tradition of Theravāda cultures. Perhaps it is without much value from a methodological or "scientific" point of view, and although admittedly it is open to a broad range of subjective interpretation, this still proved to be an interesting experiment. It revealed a wide spectrum of opinion, indicative of the fact that Buddhist doctrine in Theravāda countries is not always fixed. Briefly, and by way of summarizing what were often lengthy and complex conversations, let me note that in general members of the monastic order (*sangha*) everywhere tend to regard all forms of desire with suspicion. This is understandable when one considers that the discipline of the monastic life (*dasasikkhāpadāni*) must resist virtually every form of desire. Consequently, the Mahasi Sayadaw of Sasana Yeiktha, Rangoon, Burma and Narada Mahathera of Vajirarama Vihara, Bambalapitiya, Sri Lanka, represent those clergy who found the argument too sharply formulated or too strong. I gathered that Narada might have been interested in a more subtle expression of the issue, but Mahasi was uncompromising in his repudiation of any worth desire might have.

A middle path was adopted by Nyanaponika Mahathera of Udawatakele, Sri Lanka, who patiently went through every shred of evidence I brought before him. He agreed that great care has to be exercised when one speaks of desire from the point of view of various levels of craving. He also felt that each Pāli word for desire had a traditional meaning. Thus, for example, he argued that in his judgment *taṇhā* was always evil (*pāpa*), a stage even more damaging than "unwholesome" (*akusala*). In the occasional passage where craving appears to take on a more positive import, Nyanaponika suggested that these were exceptions to the rule. In effect, he preferred to set them aside for that reason. Piyadassi Thera of Bambalapitiya, Sri Lanka, thought that my interpretation was a little unusual, but although he had reservations about the positive power of craving, he expressed lively interest in the argument. Among informed lay Buddhists there was far more willingness to see the constructive role of desire, even in the spiritual life. I found general agreement on this point from Professor Lily de Silva of the Department of Pāli and Professor M. W. P. de Silva of the Department of Philosophy, Peradeniya, Sri Lanka, and from Professors Chayan Vaddhanaphuti and Sulak Sivaraksa of Chiengmai and Thammasat Universities, Thailand.

19. The dual connotation of *chanda* is clearly brought out, for example, in the indexes for the Saṃyutta Nikāya, VI, 38, where the many references to *chanda* are listed under the two broad headings, "the exercise of *chanda* as essential to salvation" and, "the extirpation of *chanda* as essential to salvation."

20. "Monks, if emphasizing desire, a monk lays hold of meditation, lays hold of one-pointedness of mind, this act is called 'desire-concentration.' He generates desire for the non-arising of unwholesome, unprofitable states that have not yet arisen, he lays hold of and exerts his mind to this end." *"Chandaṃ ce bhikkhave bhikkhu nissāya labhati samādhiṃ labhati cittassa ekaggataṃ ayam vuccati chandasamādhi. So anuppannānam pāpakānam akusalānaṃ dhammānam anuppādāya chandaṃ janeti vāyamati viriyam*

ārabhati cittam pagaṇhāti padahati." S.5.268.

21. C. A. F. Rhys Davids, Compendium of Philosophy, trans. by Shwe Zan Aung (London: Luzac, 1963), 244. See also Lama Govinda, The Psychological Attitude of Early Buddhist Philosophy (London: Rider Press, 1961), 119f.
22. G. P. Malalasekera, "Some Aspects of Buddhism," in S. Yamaguchi, ed., Buddhism and Culture (Kyoto: Nakana, 1960), 62.
23. K. N. Jayatilleke, Buddhism and Peace (Kandy: B.P.S., 1969), 12.
24. Cf. The parable of the goad (A.2.115). Commenting on this passage H. V. Guenther writes, "only by energy (*viriya*) can we obtain the goal. *Viriyam* is the behaviour and activity of the energetic man...energy is not just physical output, but that which permeates the whole attitude or mental outlook of man dealing with the problems to attain spiritual maturity... It is will-power." Philosophy and Pscyhology in the Adhidhamma, 200f.
25. Pali English Dictionary (London: Luzac, 1966), 322.
26. H. Saddhatissa, Buddhist Ethics (London: Allen, Unwin, 1970), 111.
27. This list totals eleven, and requires further explanation. The "fifth" virtue of intemperance is not found in all lists of the *dasa-sīla* (viz. S.4.342). It is, however, presupposed as a condition for the monastic life, along with other "steps of training" (*sikkhāpada*) such as not eating after midday, and refraining from dancing and entertainment, from adornment and cosmetics, from high beds and from handling money. See Nyanatiloka Bhikkhu, Buddhist Dictionary (Colombo: Frewin Press, 1956), 155; and the Pāli English Dictionary, P.T.S., 712.
28. G. Grimm, The Doctrine of the Buddha (Delhi: Motilal Banarsidass, 1973), Chapter 4.
29. J. Kornfield, Living Buddhist Masters (Santa Cruz: Unity Press, 1979).

30. R. Robinson, The Buddhist Religion (Belmont: Dickenson Press, 1970), 27.
31. W. L. King, Theravāda Meditation: The Buddhist Transformation of Yoga (University Park: Pennsylvania University Press, 1980), 6.
32. Nyanaponika Thera, The Heart of Buddhist Meditation (London: Rider Press, 1969), 63.
33. Swearer, Secrets of the Lotus, 51.
34. Pali-English Dictionary, 286.
35. E. Conze, Buddhist Meditation (London: Allen, Unwin, 1959), 32: "If the subject (*samādhi*) fails to come to life, it is perhaps because the secret, known two thousand years ago, has, with so much else, been lost in the meantime. It may also be because the ancient authorities believed in not being very explicit about mental states which only experience, and no description, can reveal."
36. Pali-English Dictionary, 286.
37. Johansson, The Psychology of Nirvana, 101.
38. An exception is apparent in Ledi Sayadaw's practice of *vipassanā*, where, as King reports, "many *jhānic* qualities are paralleled, and the *jhānic* flavour in *vipassanā* is present even though *jhānic* attainments have been specifically forsworn." Theravāda Meditation, 136.
39. Nyanaponika, The Heart of Buddhist Meditation, 30.
40. Swearer, Secrets of the Lotus, 40.
41. King, Theravāda Meditation, 138.
42. A. B. Keith, Buddhist Philosophy in India and Ceylon (Varanasi: Chowkhamba Series, 1963), 33.
43. C. A. Moore, "Buddhism and Science: Both Sides," Buddhism and Culture, 103f.
44. E. Conze, Buddhist Meditation (London: Allen, Unwin, 1959), 24.
45. H. D. Lewis, World Religions (London: Watts, 1966), 164.
46. Keith, Buddhist Philosophy in India and Ceylon, 33.
47. Conze, Buddhist Meditation, 32.
48. Lewis, World Religions, 164.

49. S. Radhakrishan, The Brahma Sūtra (London: Allen, Unwin, 1960), 117.
50. G. P. Malalasekera, "Buddhism and the Race Question" (Paris: UNESCO Publication, 1958), 11.
51. C. Humphreys, Buddhism (London: Penguin Books, 1951), 222.
52. A. K. Warder, "Early Buddhism and Other Contemporary Systems," Bulletin of the School of Oriental and African Studies 18 (1956), 57.
53. Johansson, Psychology of Nirvana, 111f.
54. Jayatilleke, Early Buddhist Theory of Knowledge, 466.
55. Ibid., 61, 418, 420, 425.
56. Ibid., 420, 466.
57. R. Johansson, The Psychology of Nirvana, 91.
58. C. A. F. Rhys Davids, Sakya, or Buddhist Origins. (London: Macmillan Press, 1931), 55.
59. R. H. L. Slater, Paradox and Nirvāṇa (Chicago: University of Chicago Press, 1951), 77.

CONCLUSION

1. The problem of craving ought not to be passed over without some remarks, however brief, concerning its place in the contemporary Buddhist world. This issue is still the focus of many *dhamma* sermons and discussions. With the rise of overt materialism in South and Southeast Asia, one wonders whether the gap may widen between what Richard Gombrich distinguishes as "cognitive" religion (what people say about their beliefs and practices) and "affective" religion (the religion of the heart expressed in actual conduct). See Precept and Practise (Oxford: Clarendon, 1971), 220. Everyday materialism, economic development, and modernity bring fundamental challenges to the traditional Buddhist world-view. This is particularly apparent in the consumer-oriented society of Thailand and, increasingly, Sri Lanka. Some Buddhists argue that new life-styles and ideologies have already contributed to rising greed and thereby undermine one of the principal

tenets of Buddhism. The Western concept of development is based on individual self-assertion and collective ambition and seems not to lend itself coherently to traditional Buddhist peoples. Others take this a step further and suggest that, for instance, because Buddhist values do not find natural expression in modern free-enterprise economies, therefore Buddhism is responsible for slow development and backward ways.

There is an obvious need for Buddhist thinkers to respond to such matters and to point the way to adapting the *dhamma* to the evolving world in which they live. Much encouraging work has already been done as Buddhists, especially in South and Southeast Asia, meet the forces of modernity with increasing awareness of the need not to be overcome by them. As expressed, for instance, in the excellent volume, Religion and Development in Asian Societies (Colombo: Marga, 1974), this is no time to preach a doctrine of passive acceptance to karmic fate or the uselessness of incentive and effort. A recent report, for example, which suggests that these are fundamental Buddhist goals and are the reasons for Burma's chronic economic malaise, prompts Trevor Ling to point out how remarkable it is that anyone claiming to expound Buddhist doctrine should fail to note that the doctrine does not discourage moral effort. See Buddhism, Imperialism and War (London: Allen, Unwin, 1979), 111.

The point here is that traditional Buddhist instruction on effort, will, and even craving has helped generations of Buddhists meet their individual and social responsibilities in diverse political and economic situations. It has not discouraged them from being materially acquisitive nor from wanting better things and conditions for themselves and others. It would be a crude misinterpretation of Buddhism to suggest that worldly development and rightful quest of a higher standard of living are to be equated with coarse *taṇhā*. What the Buddha has given in this great teaching is a middle way which, if carefully and seriously followed, resolves the problem of craving and painfulness while not ignoring the human dimensions of natural want and ethical responsibility.

INDEX OF TECHNICAL TERMS

SR SUPPLEMENTS

1. **FOOTNOTES TO A THEOLOGY**
   The Karl Barth Colloquium of 1972
   Edited and Introduced by Martin Rumscheidt
   1974 / viii + 151 pp. / OUT OF PRINT
2. **MARTIN HEIDEGGER'S PHILOSOPHY OF RELIGION**
   John R. Williams
   1977 / x + 190 pp. / $8.00 (paper). In U.S.A. $9.25 (paper)
3. **MYSTICS AND SCHOLARS**
   The Calgary Conference on Mysticism 1976
   Edited by Harold Coward and Terence Penelhum
   1977 / viii + 121 pp. / AVAILABLE IN LIMITED QUANTITY
4. **GOD'S INTENTION FOR MAN**
   Essays in Christian Anthropology
   William O. Fennell
   1977 / xii + 56 pp. / $2.50 (paper). In U.S.A. $3.00 (paper)
5. **"LANGUAGE" IN INDIAN PHILOSOPHY AND RELIGION**
   Edited and Introduced by Harold G. Coward
   1978 / x + 98 pp. / $5.50 (paper). In U.S.A. $6.50 (paper)
6. **BEYOND MYSTICISM**
   James R. Horne
   1978 / vi + 158 pp. / $6.50 (paper). In U.S.A. $7.50 (paper)
7. **THE RELIGIOUS DIMENSION OF SOCRATES' THOUGHT**
   James Beckman
   1979 / xii + 276 pp. / OUT OF PRINT
8. **NATIVE RELIGIOUS TRADITIONS**
   Edited by Earle H. Waugh and K. Dad Prithipaul
   1979 / xii + 244 pp. / OUT OF PRINT
9. **DEVELOPMENTS IN BUDDHIST THOUGHT**
   Canadian Contributions to Buddhist Studies
   Edited by Roy C. Amore
   1979 / iv + 196 pp. / $6.95 (paper). In U.S.A. $8.25 (paper)
10. **THE BODHISATTVA DOCTRINE IN BUDDHISM**
    Edited and Introduced by Leslie S. Kawamura
    1981 / xxii + 274 pp. / $6.95 (paper). In U.S.A. $8.25 (paper)
11. **POLITICAL THEOLOGY IN THE CANADIAN CONTEXT**
    Edited by Benjamin G. Smillie
    1982 / xii + 260 pp. / $6.50 (paper). In U.S.A. $7.50 (paper)
12. **TRUTH AND COMPASSION**
    Essays on Judaism and Religion in Memory of Rabbi Dr. Solomon Frank
    Edited by Howard Joseph, Jack N. Lightstone, and Michael D. Oppenheim
    1983 / vi + 217 pp. / $8.95 (paper). In U.S.A. $10.50 (paper)
13. **CRAVING AND SALVATION**
    A Study in Buddhist Soteriology
    Bruce Matthews
    1983 / xiv + 138 pp. / $6.50 (paper). In U.S.A. $7.50 (paper)

EDITIONS SR

1. **LA LANGUE DE YA'UDI**
   Description et classement de l'ancien parler de Zencirci dans le cadre des langues sémitiques du nord-ouest
   Paul-Eugène Dion, O.P.
   1974 / viii + 511 p. / $9.00 (paper). In U.S.A. $10.50 (paper)
2. **THE CONCEPTION OF PUNISHMENT IN EARLY INDIAN LITERATURE**
   Terence P. Day
   1982 / iv + 328 pp. / $7.00 (paper). In U.S.A. $8.00 (paper)
3. **TRADITIONS IN CONTACT AND CHANGE**
   Selected Proceedings of the XIVth Congress of the International Association for the History of Religions
   Edited by Peter Slater and Donald Wiebe with Maurice Boutin and Harold Coward
   1983 / x + 758 pp. / $14.50 (paper). In U.S.A. $16.75 (paper)

STUDIES IN CHRISTIANITY AND JUDAISM / ETUDES SUR LE CHRISTIANISME ET LE JUDAISME

1. **A STUDY IN ANTI-GNOSTIC POLEMICS**
   Irenaeus, Hippolytus, and Epiphanius
   Gérard Vallée
   1981 / xii + 114 pp. / $5.00 (paper). In U.S.A. $5.75 (paper)

THE STUDY OF RELIGION IN CANADA / SCIENCES RELIGIEUSES AU CANADA

1. **RELIGIOUS STUDIES IN ALBERTA**
   A State-of-the-Art Review
   Ronald W. Neufeldt
   1983 / xiv + 145 pp. / $8.50 (paper). In U.S.A. $10.00 (paper)

Also published / Avons aussi publié

RELIGION AND CULTURE IN CANADA / RELIGION ET CULTURE AU CANADA
Edited by / sous la direction de
Peter Slater
1977 / viii + 568 pp. / $8.50 (paper). In U.S.A. $9.75 (paper)

Available from / en vente chez:

WILFRID LAURIER UNIVERSITY PRESS
Wilfrid Laurier University
Waterloo, Ontario, Canada N2L 3C5

Published for the
Canadian Corporation for Studies in Religion/
Corporation Canadienne des Sciences Religieuses
by Wilfrid Laurier University Press